Postwar Europe: A Very Short Introduction

VERY SHORT INTRODUCTIONS are for anyone wanting a stimulating and accessible way into a new subject. They are written by experts, and have been translated into more than 45 different languages.

The series began in 1995, and now covers a wide variety of topics in every discipline. The VSI library currently contains over 750 volumes—a Very Short Introduction to everything from Psychology and Philosophy of Science to American History and Relativity—and continues to grow in every subject area.

Very Short Introductions available now:

For more information visit our website

www.oup.com/vsi/

Richard Bessel

POSTWAR EUROPE

A Very Short Introduction

OXFORD
UNIVERSITY PRESS

OXFORD
UNIVERSITY PRESS

Great Clarendon Street, Oxford, OX2 6DP,
United Kingdom

Oxford University Press is a department of the University of Oxford.
It furthers the University's objective of excellence in research, scholarship,
and education by publishing worldwide. Oxford is a registered trade mark of
Oxford University Press in the UK and in certain other countries

Published in the United States of America by Oxford University Press
198 Madison Avenue, New York, NY 10016, United States of America

British Library Cataloguing in Publication Data

Data available

Library of Congress Control Number: 2024952966

ISBN 9780198851660

Printed and bound by
CPI Group (UK) Ltd., Croydon, CR0 4YY

Links to third party websites are provided by Oxford in good faith and
for information only. Oxford disclaims any responsibility for the materials
contained in any third party website referenced in this work.

The manufacturer's authorised representative in the EU for product safety is Oxford
University Press España S.A. of El Parque Empresarial San Fernando de Henares, Avenida
de Castilla, 2 – 28830 Madrid (www.oup.es/en or product.safety@oup.com). OUP España
S.A. also acts as importer into Spain of products made by the manufacturer.

Preface

Postwar Europe is a vast topic. To write a 'Very Short Introduction' of the postwar history of the European continent is a challenging undertaking. All the more so due to the range of subjects it involves—from geopolitics and economics to demographic trends and cultural life—and the enormous literature that it has generated. Given the present format it is inevitable that many aspects are dealt with in an abbreviated manner and that others have been omitted. Some key subjects are discussed in greater detail in other 'Very Short Introductions'—notably Robert McMahon's *The Cold War* and Simon Usherwood and John Pinder's *The European Union*. The aim here is to present a concise, accessible, and broad overview that offers both a general account of postwar Europe and some interpretative paths through its multifaceted history.

All history writing reflects the time and place when it was written. Had this slim volume been written two decades ago, it would have been framed by a different understanding of where its subject was headed. It would have been framed from a more optimistic standpoint—one of an apparently and largely successful if often painful emergence from a deeply disturbing and destructive past. At the time when this volume was being drafted, however, the period of relative peace in Europe (although not in Europe's erstwhile colonies), when major military conflict between

European states appeared a thing of the past, could be seen as an aberration. The pessimism of the present colours our understanding of Europe's recent past.

It is obvious that I have been dependent in this undertaking on the findings and insights of innumerable researchers and observers, and have profited from discussions with friends and colleagues who know much more about specific aspects of this topic than I. Special thanks must go to John Breuilly, Martin Geyer, and Pavel Kolář, who read through the entire draft and offered most helpful suggestions for improvement, and to a particularly thoughtful anonymous reader whose detailed comments have been extremely valuable.

Contents

List of illustrations

List of maps

List of abbreviations

AFN	American Forces Network
BMW	Bavarian Motor Works (*Bayerische Motoren Werke*)
CDU	Christian Democratic Union (*Christlich Demokratische Union*)
CGT	General Confederation of Labour (*Confédération Générale du Travail*)
CIA	Central Intelligence Agency
CMEA	Council for Mutual Economic Assistance
CND	Campaign for Nuclear Disarmament
CRS	Republican Security Corps (*Compagnies républicaines de sécurité*)
DGB	German Trade Union Federation (*Deutscher Gewerkschaftsbund*)
DM	German Mark (*Deutsche Mark*)
DP	Displaced Person
EC	European Community
ECSC	European Coal and Steel Community
EDC	European Defence Community
EEC	European Economic Community
ETA	Basque Homeland and Freedom (*Euzkadi Ta Askatasuna*)

EU	European Union
FLN	National Libération Front (*Front de libération nationale*)
FRG	Federal Republic of Germany
GDP	Gross Domestic Product
GDR	German Democratic Republic
GM	General Motors
HLM	Dwellings for Moderate Rent (*habitations à loyer modéré*)
ILO	International Labour Organization
KPB	Communist Party of Belgium (*Kommunistische Partij van België*)
KPD	Communist Party of Germany (*Kommunistische Partei Deutschlands*)
NATO	North Atlantic Treaty Organization
NHS	National Health Service
NKVD	People's Commissariat for Internal Affairs (Народный комиссариат внутренних дел, *Narodnyy komissariat vnutrennikh del*)
OAS	Secret Army Organization (*Organisation de l'armée secrète*)
OKW	High Command of the Armed Forces (*Oberkommando der Wehrmacht*)
OPEC	Organization of the Petroleum Exporting Countries
PCB	Belgian Communist Party (*Parti communiste belge*)
PCF	French Communist Party (*Parti communiste français*)
PCI	Italian Communist Party (*Partito Comunista Italiano*)
POW	prisoner of war
PSI	Italian Socialist Party (*Partito Socialista Italiano*)
RSFSR	Russian Soviet Federative Socialist Republic

SAP	Swedish Social Democratic Labour Party (*Sveriges Socialdemokratiska Arbetareparti*)
SBZ	Soviet Occupation Zone (*Sowjetische Besatzungszone*)
SED	Socialist Unity Party of Germany (*Sozialistische Einheitspartei Deutschlands*)
SHAEF	Supreme Headquarters, Allied Expeditionary Force
SVP/UDC	Swiss People's Party (Schweizerische Volkspartei/ *Union démocratique du centre, Unione Democratica di Centro*)
SWAPO	South West Africa People's Organization
UDI	Unilateral Declaration of Independence
UK	United Kingdom
UN	United Nations
UNESCO	United Nations Educational, Scientific and Cultural Organization
UNRRA	United Nations Relief and Rehabilitation Administration
US(A)	United States (of America)
USSR	Union of Soviet Socialist Republics
WTO	Warsaw Treaty Organization

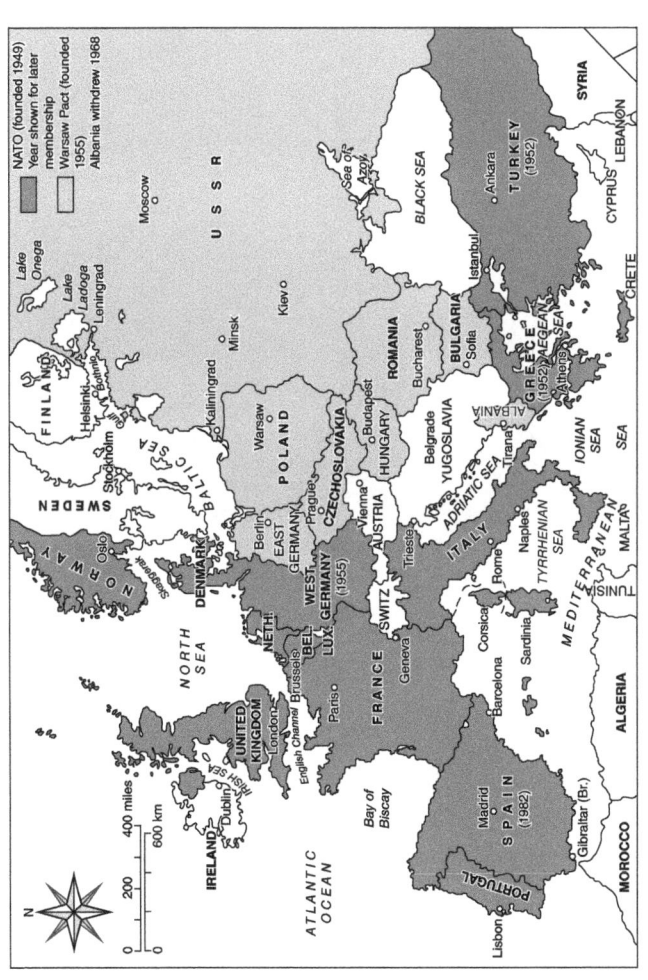

Map 1. Europe 1945–89.

Chapter 1
What was postwar Europe?

The Second World War was the most destructive conflict in human history. While it was a global conflict, the majority of those who lost their lives were European. By the time Germany surrendered in May 1945, the continent was in ruins, tens of millions were dead, and tens of millions more injured, disabled, or uprooted. Europe's economies were gravely damaged and millions of its people faced homelessness, malnutrition, or worse. Europe's political systems had been shaken and, in many places, destroyed; democratic government had been crushed across most of the continent; millions of people were in uniform, occupying countries not their own, and millions more found themselves in prisoner-of-war camps. The prospects for postwar Europe looked bleak, and Europeans had somehow to dig themselves out of a hole of unprecedented depth.

A quarter of a century later the European continent presented a very different picture. Its economies had recovered and grown phenomenally, and Europe appeared generally to be politically stable, albeit divided by the Cold War. Democratic government had been re-established or established in western Europe, then in southern Europe. Europe's inhabitants were for the most part well housed and well fed and generally enjoyed a physically secure existence and the benefits of a developed welfare state.

Then in the late 1980s and early 1990s the political, military, and economic division of the continent ended as the eastern half of the continent experienced political and economic revolution. The framework that had taken shape in the aftermath of the Second World War disintegrated, and a new chapter in Europe's history had begun.

Europe's postwar was an age of optimism. After the tsunami of violence during the first half of the 20th century, an armed peace descended on the continent; after the economic stagnation and catastrophic depression of the interwar period, the continent enjoyed unprecedented economic growth that, for a short period of time, seemed might continue forever. In a rather shabby iteration, parallel beliefs held sway in the eastern half of the continent, where self-styled victors of history were committed to creating a socialist utopia on the ruins left by fascism and war. Although the 1950s and 1960s witnessed a succession of political and economic crises, many people nevertheless could believe that a brave new world was unfolding. Then, after Europe's postwar 'golden age' began to fade and was followed by the dismal decade of the 1970s, the collapse of 'real-existing socialism' in eastern Europe gave postwar optimism a new lease on life. Political and economic liberty had triumphed, or so it seemed.

In the 21st century, however, with the rise of populist nationalism across the continent and open military conflict, that optimism has evaporated. In May 2019, on the 74th anniversary of Victory in Europe Day, Timothy Garton Ash warned (in a statement even more prescient than he could have imagined at the time): 'Seven decades after the end of the second world war on European soil, the Europe we have built since then is under attack.' The confidence with which many Europeans had faced the future during the postwar years seems a distant memory.

Writing some two decades earlier, in a more optimistic time, Tony Judt asserted that Europe had become 'more conscious of its twentieth-century history than at any time in the past fifty years'. However, at the same time he stated that 'Europe is not re-entering its troubled past—on the contrary, it is leaving it', remarking that 'Postwar in Europe lasted a very long time, but it is finally coming to a close.' Now Postwar Europe indeed has come to a close and, consequently, it should be possible to view its history from beginning to end.

Yet it is far from clear when 'Postwar Europe' began and when it ended. When and where was 'Postwar Europe'? While the German surrender in May 1945 may appear to have signalled the end of the Second World War in Europe, for many millions of Europeans that was hardly so. On the one hand, in many places in Europe the war had ended well before the Wehrmacht capitulated. For most of France the fighting was over by the end of 1944 once Allied armies had liberated the country following the D-Day invasion in June; the Provisional Government of the French Republic, established at the beginning of June 1944 with Charles de Gaulle at its head, moved its capital from Algiers to Paris on 31 August, a few days after the city's liberation, and in effect comprised a postwar government in wartime. In Germany, Allied armies had arrived and the fighting had ceased in much of the country during the weeks before May 1945; Aachen, the first major German city to be captured by the Allies, fell to American forces in October 1944. In much of eastern Europe—in Russia, Ukraine, Belarus, Poland, Romania, Bulgaria—German forces had been swept away well before Germany accepted defeat. And, of course, Europe included states that had not been combatants during the Second World War: Ireland, Sweden, Switzerland, Spain, and Portugal.

On the other hand, war in Europe did not cease abruptly on 8 May 1945. Numerous conflicts raged on the continent long after Germany surrendered—in Poland, Yugoslavia, Greece, Moldavia, Ukraine, the Baltic countries of Estonia, Latvia, and Lithuania. This all makes it difficult to say precisely when wartime ceased and postwar began.

Yet more difficult is to determine when the postwar era came to an end. Can it be said to have ended abruptly with the political and military division of Europe in the late 1940s, when the wartime alliance that had defeated the Axis powers fractured and Europe divided into hostile camps facing each other along what Winston Churchill referred to in March 1946 in Fulton, Missouri, as the 'Iron Curtain'? Did it end with the suppression of popular revolts in eastern Europe in 1953 and 1956, or with the construction of the Berlin Wall in August 1961 and the subsequent apparent stabilization of the Soviet bloc? Did it come to a close with the economic recovery that set in during the 1950s and brought unprecedented prosperity at least to western Europe in the 1960s, or with the economic crisis that followed from the oil-price shock of 1973 and ended the longest and strongest economic boom in modern European history? Did the postwar era end with the collapse of state-socialist dictatorships in the eastern half of the continent and the subsequent changes in (eastern) Europe's postwar borders, or with the outbreak of the Balkan Wars of the 1990s? Or has it only come to an end with the disintegration of political cultures consolidated in Europe after 1945, or with the outbreak of a major land war in Europe in February 2022?

To make matters yet more complicated, it is also less than clear what and where comprised 'postwar Europe'. Obviously those countries that were combatants and/or were occupied during the Second World War should be included within this frame, but how are we to consider European countries that were neutral and therefore not directly involved in that war? Ireland, Portugal, Spain, Sweden, and Switzerland were not drawn directly into the Second World War, yet they were greatly affected by it and were shaped by many of the same developments after 1945 as were countries that had been involved directly in military conflict. Spain had had its own war, the Spanish Civil War, and so for Spain 'postwar' meant something rather different than it did for other European states. The European countries that had remained neutral during the Second World War were affected profoundly by the economic boom of the 1950s and 1960s, by the cultural transformations of the postwar years, and by the demographic shifts across Europe during the second half of the 20th century.

Furthermore, the story of 'postwar Europe' is not limited to the European continent. The development of postwar Europe, essentially of western Europe, was entangled with the lands in Asia and Africa that achieved independence from European states after the Second World War. This process then reshaped European societies, in large measure due to immigration from former colonies. Thus Europe's postwar history is not least a history of 'Europe after empire'.

The postwar era may also be delineated through the frame of memory. This refers not simply to the period during which there remained a substantial number of people who had experienced the Second World War, either on the military front or on the home front. It also refers to the period during which memories of the war—real or imagined—occupied a central place in the public consciousness of Europeans, whether or not they experienced the war years themselves. This is not just a matter of remembering, but also of forgetting. Tony Judt asserted that 'Europe's post-war history is a story shadowed by silences; by absence', that 'without such collective amnesia, Europe's astonishing post-war recovery would not have been possible', and that 'silence over Europe's recent past was the necessary condition for the construction of a European future'.

That 'European future' is now the European past, and the story of Europe after 1945 is a multifaceted history of its politics, economies, societies, and people. Underpinning this 'Very Short Introduction' is the fact that the Second World War left behind tens of millions of dead, injured, homeless, uprooted, and bereaved human beings across the European continent. The story of postwar Europe is their story: the story of the people who lived through the Second World War and have now largely passed away, and of their children, the postwar generations who have retired or are approaching retirement—of the Europeans who lived their lives in the wake of the greatest conflict that the world had seen.

Chapter 2
The end of the Second World War in Europe

'On the day of peace I remember my mother standing and
making the bed in the bedroom, the window was open
and the ringing of church bells could be heard. From our
big Telefunken radio we could hear the broadcast about
Germany's capitulation. My mother said:

—Now it's over at last.'

On 3 May 1945, Admiral Karl Dönitz, the man Hitler had named
as his successor before committing suicide, sent the commander-in-
chief of the Navy, Admiral Hans-Georg von Friedeburg, to meet
British Field Marshal Bernard Montgomery on Lüneburg Heath to
agree the surrender of German forces in 'the north-western area'.
On 4 May von Friedeburg signed the surrender document at
Montgomery's headquarters, and at 8:00 a.m. on 5 May fighting
ceased in north-western Germany, the Netherlands, and Denmark.
Friedeburg then attempted to secure a similar arrangement with
the western allies' supreme commander, General Dwight
Eisenhower, at Reims. When Eisenhower refused to countenance a
partial surrender and demanded a complete, immediate, and
unconditional surrender, the Germans had no choice but to agree.
At 2:41 a.m. on 7 May *Generaloberst* (Colonel General) Alfred Jodl
signed the surrender document on behalf of the *Oberkommando
der Wehrmacht* (OKW, High Command of the Armed Forces), and

at midnight on the night of 8/9 May the Second World War in Europe formally came to an end. (Just after midnight, on 9 May, the capitulation ceremony was played out again, this time in Karlshorst in eastern Berlin and with a full surrender document and representatives of the forces of the USSR, the USA, the UK, and France present; as the ceremony had been scheduled to begin earlier, the Karlshorst surrender document bore the date 8 May 1945.) Although fighting continued to the east of Prague until 11 May, and although all German forces in Yugoslavia did not surrender until the 15th, Germany's Second World War was over.

The end of the conflict was greeted with jubilation among those who had fought against or been subjugated by Germany, and with relief among many who had been on the losing side (Figures 1a and 1b). Nevertheless, there were numerous military confrontations in Europe after May 1945: anti-communist resistance in Poland, where fighting continued until the end of 1947; civil war in Greece

1a. Victory celebrations in Moscow, 1945.

1b. Victory celebrations in London, May 1945.

until 1949 that caused greater loss of life than had the German occupation during the Second World War and left roughly a tenth of the entire population homeless; armed resistance against the Soviet Union in Moldavia from 1944 until 1953, whereby roughly one in 20 of the total population died from starvation; the guerrilla war of the 'Forest Brothers' in the Baltic countries Estonia, Latvia, and (most heavily) Lithuania, a war that cost roughly 50,000 people their lives and lasted until the early 1950s. In Ukraine, where the 'Insurgent Army' fought against the Soviet state during the late 1940s (during a famine that cost the lives of perhaps over a million people), and in Yugoslavia, where bloody ethnic cleansing of the German minorities and continuing warfare left tens of thousands of victims, warfare raged well after the Second World War had ended. In addition, conflict involving Europeans erupted beyond Europe, where the bloody postwar history of the end of European empires had begun.

Where military conflict had ceased in Europe after the German defeat, the violence unleashed by the Second World War nevertheless continued to reverberate, as the experiences and crimes of the years 1939–45 led to prosecutions of alleged collaborators and war criminals and to thousands of extra-judicial, summary executions. In France the *épuration* ('purification') following liberation resulted in between 10,000 and 11,000 deaths, of which more than 80 per cent were the result of summary executions (*exécutions extra-judiciaires*). In Italy, roughly 10,000 people met their deaths in the postwar purges. In Denmark, where capital punishment had been abolished in 1933 (and no executions had taken place since the 1890s), the death penalty was reinstated in 1945 in order to deal with wartime collaborators; there 76 people were sentenced to death, of whom 46 were executed by firing squad; the total number killed, when extra-legal reprisals are included, was many times that number. In Norway, where the death penalty had been abolished in 1902, it was reinstated immediately after liberation in 1945 and executions were carried out until 1948. In the Netherlands, where the post-1945 purge of wartime collaborators (in order to expunge what Prime Minister Willem Schermerhorn described in a radio address in June 1945 as a 'cancerous tumour in our nation'), nearly 100,000 were interned and 152 people received death sentences, 40 of whom were executed. In Belgium, where the reckoning was carried out proportionally even more harshly than in France or in the Netherlands, 242 people (237 of whom were Belgians) were executed after the war.

Even greater retribution occurred in eastern Europe, where it was used to crush resistance to the new postwar political order. In Bulgaria, more than 1,500 people were executed. In Czechoslovakia, where the expulsion of the German population after the war was carried out in a brutal manner, it has been estimated that in 1945 between 19,000 and 30,000 Germans were killed as a result of 'vigilantism'; in addition, before the communists came to power in the coup of February 1948 almost 700 people were executed after being tried in court. Worse occurred in Yugoslavia, where the postwar violence included mass shootings, in the first instance of supporters of the Croatian Ustaše and Slovenian collaborators; the number of victims has been estimated at 70,000. In the Soviet Union, huge numbers of 'Displaced Persons' returned after the war to face repression: according to Soviet statistics, by March 1946 roughly 6.5 per cent of the millions of 'DPs' who had returned to the Soviet Union after May 1945, often against their will, were referred 'to the NKVD' (the People's Commissariat for Internal Affairs—i.e. in all probability killed), and 14.48 per cent were conscripted into forced-labour battalions immediately upon their arrival back in the USSR.

The continuing violence occurred on a continent where civil society had been deeply damaged and, in some places, shattered. Millions of 'foreign workers', who had been carried off to work in Germany's war economy, had been liberated, and not a few used the opportunity to exact revenge against their erstwhile masters. In Poland during the early postwar years the 'recovered territories', which had been Germany's eastern Prussian provinces, were referred to with good reason as 'Poland's Wild West' (*Polski Dziki Zachód*). In Hungary a collapse of the old state institutions, a catastrophic economic situation, and hyperinflation led to a wave of criminality, above all in Budapest. Violence against Jews did not end with the collapse of National Socialist Germany: anti-Jewish outrages occurred after the war in Hungary, Slovakia, and, most notably, Poland—which saw the worst example of the postwar anti-Semitic violence with the pogrom on 4 July 1946 in Kielce in southern Poland, which left over 40 people dead. In the aftermath of war people across the European continent faced displacement, expropriation, reprisals, purges, summary executions, pogroms, rape, and public humiliation.

This took place as millions of Europeans were expelled from their homes. Rather than borders being drawn around existing patterns of ethnic settlement as after the First World War, after the Second World War borders were drawn and groups of people were moved to conform to them. In July and August 1945 formal agreement was reached at Potsdam about the supposedly provisional borders of a postwar Germany (ceding substantial territory to postwar Poland and the USSR) and about the 'transfer to Germany of German populations, or elements thereof, remaining in Poland, Czechoslovakia, and Hungary', stipulating that 'any transfers that take place should be effected in an orderly and humane manner'. This was window dressing. Neither were the expulsions 'effected in an orderly and humane manner' nor did they begin only after being sanctioned in the Potsdam Agreement: the 'wild' expulsions of Germans from Czechoslovakia and Poland were well under way before the Agreement was finalized.

For countries that had fought on Germany's side at one point or another—Italy, Hungary, Romania, Finland, and Bulgaria—it was the Paris Peace Treaty, ratified on 10 February 1947, that fixed their postwar frontiers. These countries were compelled to cede territory gained during the war, and then some: Italy lost its colonies in Africa (Libya and Italian East Africa), and had to cede Istria (including the provinces of Fiume and Zara) to Yugoslavia; Finland was restored to its borders at the beginning of 1941, thus confirming its losses of territory after the Winter War of 1939–40 with the USSR and nullifying its territorial gains as an ally of Germany between 1941 and 1944; Hungary lost the territorial gains it had made from 1938, returning territory to Yugoslavia, Czechoslovakia, and Romania; Romania was restored essentially to its borders as of the beginning of 1941, thus losing Bessarabia and Northern Bukovina to the USSR, but regaining Northern Transylvania from Hungary; and Bulgaria also was restored to its borders of 1 January 1941, which meant returning territory to Yugoslavia and Greece.

In some countries—Sweden, Switzerland, Great Britain, and Ireland—political order and social and economic structures largely had been preserved, governmental and civic institutions largely remained intact, and the rhythms of daily life could continue more or less as before. However, Europe in general was an exhausted continent. Many Europeans emerged too tired, too weak, and too preoccupied with everyday problems to engage actively with the wider world. For example, in October 1945 a German communist in Berlin, speaking with returning prisoners of war, observed 'how demoralized these people are' and how they focused essentially on their day-to-day material concerns. Similarly, in Poland's 'Wild West' despair and apathy were widespread among a population that had been forced from what had been eastern Poland to the 'recovered territories' in the west. Across a war-ravaged continent, Europeans retreated into their private sphere.

Societies that had been overwhelmed by people in uniform began to acquire a more civilian face, as millions of surviving soldiers were released from POW camps or demobilized. The demobilization of the Allied armies unfolded rather quickly. At the end of the Second World War the British armed forces numbered roughly five million members; of these, nearly 1.5 million had been released by the end of 1945, and another 2.5 million returned to civilian life in 1946. France, which had managed to assemble an army of some 1.3 million between the country's liberation in 1944 and Germany's capitulation in 1945, saw large numbers of them demobilized in the year that followed. When Germany surrendered, there were roughly three million American soldiers in Europe, many of whom were earmarked for redeployment in the Pacific. However, the surrender of Japan in August 1945 led to a rapid demobilization (with a million US soldiers being discharged in December 1945 alone), and by the middle of 1947 the *entire* armed forces of the USA worldwide numbered a little over 1.5 million. In the Soviet Union, the state with by far the largest armed forces in Europe, huge numbers of its soldiers were demobilized between July and September 1945, and their demobilization was largely completed by late 1947.

Many prisoners of war also were able to return home quickly: of the million and a half French soldiers who had been taken prisoner, almost all returned during April, May, and June 1945.

For German POWs, the story was more complicated. The British and, particularly, the Americans, were keen to release large numbers quickly, and consequently many of their prisoners were set free during 1945. Those who landed in French and, particularly, Soviet captivity tended to be less fortunate: perhaps 700,000 of those taken prisoner by Soviet forces died in captivity (although estimates vary greatly), and many of those who survived would spend years as prisoners, returning to Germany or Austria in the late 1940s or even the early 1950s (with the last ones arriving in 1956). Among the most unfortunate were the Soviet soldiers who had managed to survive the terrible conditions of German captivity only to find themselves accused of having surrendered and then delivered into Soviet prison camps.

Europe contained millions who had experienced war in uniform, generations of war veterans who then returned to civilian life and in many respects were to define the postwar era. Tens of millions more Europeans had survived terrible hardship, which would mark them for the rest of their lives. While conflict in Europe did not cease abruptly or neatly with Germany's capitulation, many Europeans could share the relief expressed by Hermann Hesse when he wrote on New Year's Day 1946:

> And this time, so it appears, the new, the welcome, the as yet so unblemished year is something quite special and important. After years of slaughter and destruction it is the first New Year night for us in which there is no war.

Chapter 3
Life after death: societies of survivors

The majority of the roughly 60 million dead that can be attributed to the Second World War met their deaths in Europe. The extent of these losses varied tremendously across the continent. Some countries emerged with relatively few war-related deaths: Denmark, Norway, and Bulgaria lost only a tiny proportion of their prewar populations, and the United Kingdom lost just under 1 per cent. At the other end of the scale, many regions in eastern Europe lost huge proportions of their prewar populations. Most extreme were the losses in constituent parts of the Soviet Union. Roughly a quarter of those who before the war had lived in Byelorussia (today's Belarus) died during the conflict, and in Ukraine one in six lost their lives—in both cases to a considerable degree a consequence of the murder of their Jewish populations. The epicentre of the Shoah, Poland, lost roughly one-sixth of the country's 1939 population—about six million people, half of whom were Jews. In absolute terms, Russians comprised the largest number of dead, nearly 14 million altogether, or roughly one in eight of the population before the German invasion. In Germany, where the great majority of the dead were military personnel, altogether over six million people—or more than 8 per cent of the country's prewar population—lost their lives.

Across Europe millions of survivors had lost husbands, lovers, parents, children, relatives, and friends, and decades would pass

2. An elderly German couple trundle along the Leipziger Strasse in Berlin with their remaining belongings, July 1945.

before the wartime losses no longer shaped European societies (Figure 2). Postwar Belarus, Lutz Niethammer has observed, was alongside the German Democratic Republic the 'most female society of Europe' in the wake of the Second World War. Not just the GDR but postwar Germany as a whole—with nearly 4.5 million German soldiers dead and roughly 10 million more sitting in prisoner-of-war camps when the war ended in Europe—emerged with a population that was disproportionately female. In October 1946 there were seven million more women than men living in occupied Germany, and for every 1,000 men aged between 25 and 30 there were 1,700 women of the same age; and in 1950 one-third of all households in West Germany were headed by a woman. Half the German population had lost at least one family member in the war; when the war ended, over a million German women were widows.

In Poland, where many women had experienced physical abuse, rape, and the death of their children, husbands, and relatives, and where many were left as the sole support of themselves and their children, the writer Irena Krzywicka described the Second World

War in 1956 as 'a grand and tragic agent in forming the single-parent family'. In the RSFSR (Russian Soviet Federative Socialist Republic) the number of children in orphanages in 1949 (381,568) was twice what it had been in 1941 (191,123), and they comprised but a fraction of the millions of children in the Soviet Union orphaned because of the war. In the USSR, of those born during the early 1920s, a huge proportion of the men were dead; communities were left without young adults, and for years after the war there were fewer young couples and fewer children (Figure 3).

Destruction caused by bombing and fighting on the ground, as well as flight and expulsion, led to huge shifts in where Europeans found themselves after the war. Some rural areas, where battles had been intense or where the population was largely expelled (e.g. in the territories 'recovered' by postwar Poland from Germany), held far fewer inhabitants than before the conflict; and some cities saw huge reductions in their populations. In the one-time Ukrainian capital of Kharkiv, whose population had grown to a million and a half before the war, two-thirds of the city's buildings were destroyed and a mere 190,000 inhabitants remained when the city was liberated from German occupation. The population of largely destroyed Warsaw fell from 1.3 million in 1939 to a mere 162,000 in January 1945; in May 1945 it had risen to just 366,000; in January 1947 it was 538,000, and when the figure reached one million in 1957—more than a decade after the end of the war—it still stood at only about three-quarters of the prewar total. The heavily bombed west German city of Cologne had 772,221 inhabitants in 1939, but at the end of February 1945 only 85,000 people remained, and in 1950 Cologne, with 594,941 inhabitants, still held only a little over three-quarters as many people as a decade earlier. While not all European cities experienced such population declines, many places in the immediate postwar period saw a temporary de-urbanization.

During the late 1930s and the 1940s more people across the world were compelled to leave their places of origin than ever before. In

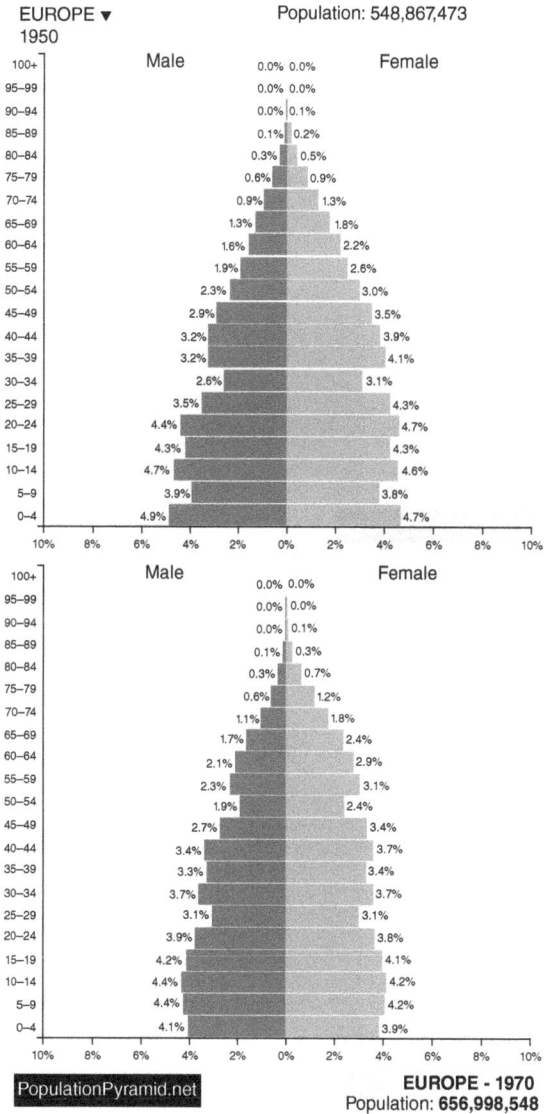

3. Europe's population in 1950, 1970, 1990, and 2000.

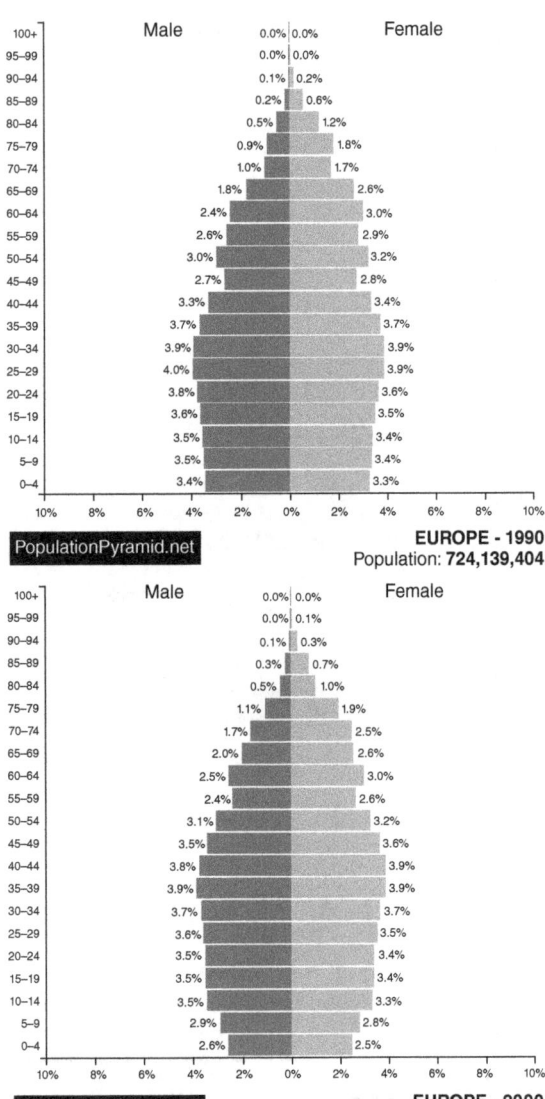

EUROPE - 1990
Population: **724,139,404**

EUROPE - 2000
Population: **728,164,208**

3. Continued.

Europe the largest number of these were the over 12 million Germans who fled or were expelled from regions of German settlement in eastern Europe. They would constitute nearly a quarter of the population of the Soviet Occupation Zone and early German Democratic Republic (GDR) and more than one in seven of the population of postwar West Germany. Further east were the more than two million Poles expelled from what had been eastern Poland or returned from deportation to Siberia and who comprised roughly 10 per cent of postwar Poland's population in 1948; they were joined by another 2.2 million Poles who had been displaced during the war by the Germans coming from the west. Deportations of Europeans continued well into the immediate postwar period. For example, roughly half a million Ukrainians were deported in 1947 from the Bieszczady region in south-eastern Poland. It has been estimated that the number of Europeans who suffered deportation as a result of the Second World War altogether probably exceeded 20 million.

An immediate challenge in 1945 was posed by the millions of DPs, non-German civilians who found themselves outside their home countries. When the war ended the numbers awaiting repatriation were huge: SHAEF, the Allied Supreme Command, estimated the number of DPs and refugees in Europe to be 11,332,700, 7,725,000 of whom were in Germany. Other estimates were even higher, suggesting that when the war came to an end there were roughly 11 million homeless people on the territory of what had been the Third Reich—former prisoners of war, forced labourers, collaborators, and people liberated from the concentration camps. From October 1945 overall responsibility for the DPs in Europe rested with the United Nations Relief and Rehabilitation Administration (UNRRA). While most were repatriated by late 1945, at the end of 1946 roughly a million (a quarter of whom were Jews) remained in the western occupation zones of Germany; in the summer of 1948 they numbered about 300,000 (80,000 of whom were Jews); and even in 1960 roughly 150,000 DPs were still living in camps and other temporary settlements in Germany, Austria, and Italy.

Due to war-related population movements and wartime campaigns of mass murder, some postwar European states were far more ethnically homogeneous than they had been before the outbreak of the war. In the Balkans between 1930 and 1950 the Jewish population fell from 856,000 to 50,000; hundreds of thousands of ethnic Germans were forced to leave Yugoslavia and Romania; and Slavs and Albanians fled northern Greece and Serbs fled Kosovo. Greater changes occurred in eastern Europe, where the murder of Jews altered the ethnic composition of Poland, Hungary, and Ukraine, and where forced removals during the war were followed by forced resettlement and deportation. Ukraine was transformed through war, mass murder, mass deportations, and postwar population transfers, creating an 'unambiguously Ukrainian nation-space' largely cleared of the ethnic minorities that had previously lived there. Postwar Poland was transformed from a multi-ethnic polity into a homogeneous nation-space through the murder of its Jewish population, the expulsion of the German population, the deportation of Ukrainians to the Soviet Union, and the physical shift of the country westwards (ceding territory, where millions of Ukrainians lived, to the USSR and gaining territory from Germany, where Poles from the east were resettled). Whereas the population of prewar Poland had been roughly two-thirds Polish with large Ukrainian, Jewish, Belorussian, and German minorities (according to the 1931 census, 68.9 per cent of the population gave Polish as their mother tongue), after 1945 the population of Poland was roughly 97 per cent Polish and Catholic.

Much of what had been the ethnically mixed Habsburg empire before the First World War was also transformed into more ethnically homogeneous nation-states after 1945. The population of Hungary, which had expanded its territory as a wartime ally of Germany and whose population within its boundaries in 1941 was roughly 80 per cent Hungarian (with substantial Romanian, Ruthenian, and German minorities as well as a large Jewish population), was almost entirely Hungarian after the Second

World War. There the wartime destruction of the country's large Jewish population was followed by the postwar expulsion to Hungary of some 300,000 Hungarians from south Slovakia, Transcarpathia, North Transylvania, and Voyvodina. (Many of these uprooted Hungarians took the place of the roughly 220,000 Germans expelled from Hungary after the war.) In Czechoslovakia, where Germans had comprised 23 per cent of its inhabitants before the war, Czechs and Slovaks together formed 90 per cent of the postwar population. The reduction in ethnic diversity within postwar European states, for all the hardship that it involved, meant that ethnic divisions that had been sources of tension and violence for decades were removed.

The border changes and population transfers meant that many communities in postwar central and eastern Europe were inhabited largely by people uprooted from elsewhere. For example, the city of Wrocław (formerly Breslau) was settled to a considerable degree by Poles from Lwów (now Lviv in Ukraine) during the early postwar years. The German population of the old Prussian capital of Königsberg was replaced by Russian inhabitants in what became Kaliningrad. In postwar West Germany people removed from Poland and Czechoslovakia established new communities—notably Neugablonz, where some 18,000 Germans from Gablonz in Czechoslovakia settled on the outskirts of Kaufbeuren in the Allgäu. The inhabitants of Stalinstadt (renamed Eisenhüttenstadt in November 1961), the new socialist industrial city built in the German Democratic Republic from 1950, consisted in large measure of 'resettlers' from the east.

Such transformations differentiated postwar eastern Europe from postwar western Europe. Whereas the populations of eastern and central Europe had borne the brunt of the human losses of Europe's Second World War and were subjected to huge population transfers, far fewer people had been killed or forced from their homes in the west of the continent during the 1940s. The postwar populations of Brussels or Bordeaux were not fundamentally different from what they had been in 1939, whereas almost all the inhabitants of postwar Wrocław and Kaliningrad were living in dwellings that former inhabitants left behind.

It would take a generation before the families of the uprooted would identify primarily with their new surroundings. Writing about the cities in western Poland settled after the war by Poles from the east, the sociologist Jan Szczepański asserted over half a century ago that

> in the twenty years that have passed [since the end of the Second World War], the problems of integration have been solved .... The milestone year of these territories was 1964, when the first children of the second-generation settlers were born there. In these twenty years, over 4 million Polish children have been born on this soil. Integration is now an accomplished fact.

A similar observation has been made for the Kaliningrad region, where the older generation consisted of Russians demobilized after the war: 'The young grew up in Kaliningrad—far from Russia—and no longer really identify with the home of their parents. Most of them know Moscow, Kazan and the Volga only from postcards.' In Germany too the younger generations, growing up far from the former homes of their parents in what had been eastern Germany and the Sudetenland, came to identify with where they lived rather than where their parents had once lived.

Wherever they were able to settle after the war, millions of Europeans had to live with damage to their health, physical and mental. In the Soviet Union in 1947 there were an estimated 16.3 million officially recognized recipients of war invalidity pensions (a number which had fallen to 3.6 million by 1975). In the Federal Republic of Germany (FRG) in 1951 war disability pensions were being paid to roughly 1.5 million people, nearly one million pensions to war widows, 1.3 million for half-orphans, and 41,000 for full-orphans; altogether, some 4,151,000 war-related pensions were being granted—of a total population of about 51 million. When the Law to Aid Victims of War (*Bundesversorgungsgesetz*) was passed in 1950—the first major piece of social legislation enacted by the FRG—it covered four million people and was the second largest item of state expenditure, exceeded only by the costs of occupation that the government had to bear.

Postwar Europe was not only inhabited by millions of survivors of the war, it was also haunted by the millions who had died. Its landscapes became dotted with war memorials dedicated to and cemeteries containing the dead of the Second World War. Some were established officially to honour the 'glorious dead'; others arose as a result of local initiatives to remember the victims of the conflict. Almost immediately after the German capitulation, the Soviet military authorities began constructing a memorial in the Tiergarten, in the middle of Berlin along the city's 'East–West Axis', behind which were to be buried the remains of some 2,500 Soviet soldiers who fell in the Battle of Berlin in the last days of the war; it was dedicated with a parade of Allied troops in November 1945. Germany contains the graves of hundreds of thousands of Soviet citizens, soldiers and civilians, with more than 350 Soviet/Russian war cemeteries in the country, mostly in the east. Within the USSR immediately after the war, simple, economical concrete stele were erected at local initiative in villages almost everywhere with the names of their inhabitants who had died in the conflict.

Germany's own war dead had to be memorialized in a low-key manner, and in the immediate postwar period public commemoration of the war dead was proscribed by the occupation powers. In May 1946 the Allied High Commission decreed that all monuments on German territory that glorified war and militarism or National Socialism were to be destroyed by the beginning of 1947, although obelisks and stele of 'local significance' for the memory of fallen soldiers, memorials for the dead of regular Wehrmacht units, and individual gravestones were allowed. Even so, in the Soviet Zone no monuments were dedicated to

Wehrmacht dead, and in western Germany when some local communities planned memorials to the war dead immediately after the war's end (paralleling what had occurred after the First World War) the applications were rejected.

In the United Kingdom, after the Second World War (as after the First) the commemoration of the war dead was organized locally. Countless British war memorials from the First World War were modified to include the names of those who had fallen in the Second. Many felt that building new stone monuments was inappropriate, preferring that resources be directed towards projects useful to the community, such as memorial public gardens (as had been established widely after 1918). For the USA the response was different, as American war dead were buried not across the Atlantic, but in various sites in Europe (but not on what had been enemy territory). Already in March 1945 the American military had established a cemetery at Saint-Avold in Lorraine, close to the German border, and later expanded it near the original site to become the largest American military cemetery of the Second World War with over 10,000 graves.

Many of the dead were never found—soldiers who had been missing in action, civilians whose bodies had been incinerated in bombing raids, people who had met their deaths in the killing fields and extermination camps. Their physical remains were missing, their fate often unknown.

The condition of the European continent and its peoples during the immediate postwar years—with millions of people mourning their dead and missing, millions of people homeless, and millions damaged physically and psychologically, in landscapes scarred by wartime destruction—did not appear to offer grounds for optimism. However, in postwar societies of survivors, millions of Europeans could look forward to peace, to rebuilding their lives, to bringing new generations into the world.

Chapter 4
New politics—east and west

On 17 July 1945, nine weeks after Germany's unconditional surrender, the heads of the governments of the UK, the USA, and the Soviet Union met in Potsdam at the Cecilienhof, a residence constructed during the First World War for the German Crown Prince Wilhelm in the style of an English Tudor manor house. The Cecilienhof had been chosen because it was one of the few places near Berlin that had escaped war damage and offered a suitable venue for a conference of world leaders. There British Prime Minister Winston Churchill, American President Harry Truman, and Chairman of the USSR Council of Ministers Joseph Stalin, accompanied by their respective foreign ministers Anthony Eden, James Byrnes, and Vyacheslav Molotov (Churchill and Eden were replaced in Potsdam after 28 July by Clement Attlee and Ernest Bevin after Churchill's Conservatives had been defeated in the British general election), set the parameters for the political map of postwar Europe (Figure 4). The immediate agenda was how defeated, occupied Germany would be administered. Drawing up peace treaties (with Italy, Romania, Bulgaria, Hungary, and Finland, which became the Paris Peace Treaties signed in 1947) would come later.

Stalin famously said in March 1944 that 'whoever occupies a territory also imposes on it his own social system. Everyone imposes his own system as far as his army can reach. It cannot be

4. Leaders of the 'big three' countries of the Anti-Hitler Coalition at the Potsdam Conference.

otherwise.' The map of postwar Europe indicates that Stalin was right: the political line of demarcation between the pluralist-capitalist west and the socialist-communist east essentially replicated the reach of the western military forces on one side and that of the Soviet Army on the other. The agreement reached in Moscow in October 1944, when Churchill and Stalin divided a map of south-eastern Europe into postwar spheres of influence, foretold the east/west divide that lasted until 1989/90.

However, although divergence of interests between the USSR and the western Allies was apparent during the war, it is doubtful whether in 1944 or 1945 Stalin had a clear idea of a postwar communist bloc being formed in eastern Europe. Communists in Eastern Europe emerged from the war aiming to build 'truly democratic' political systems based on broad coalitions (a policy that corresponded to Moscow's political line at the end of the war). The defeat of fascism and the dawn of the postwar era seemed to offer the opportunity to create a democratic order, not necessarily to impose a communist revolution. In many respects the possibilities for eastern Europe's postwar trajectory after 1945 initially seemed rather fluid. It was 1948 that proved to be what Matyas Rákosi, Hungary's postwar Stalinist ruler, described as 'the year of the turn'.

While the extent of territory reached by Soviet armed forces in the east and those of the USA, the UK, and their allies in the west would prove decisive, prospects on either side of the divide were very different. Whereas in western Europe governments-in-exile could aim to return from London and attempt to pick up where they had left off at the beginning of the war, in eastern Europe the avalanche of wartime violence had swept away the old political order. In eastern Europe prewar political structures could not be resuscitated; the question was what would replace them. There the late 1940s saw the creation of 'people's democracies' in what became (apart from Yugoslavia) the Soviet bloc.

There were four general paths to Soviet-style dictatorship in eastern Europe, each determined roughly by how a particular country emerged from the war. One group, consisting of Czechoslovakia (at least the Czech lands) and Poland, had been occupied by the Third Reich; their postwar path was one of reasserting national independence after occupation. A second group—consisting of Hungary, Romania, Bulgaria, and what in 1949 became the GDR—had fought against the Allies (the USSR); their postwar path was one of rejecting their immediate past (including the abolition of monarchies in Romania and Bulgaria). A third group, consisting of Yugoslavia and Albania, emerged with a communist leadership that owed its position to the partisan struggle against the German and Italian occupiers; consequently their postwar path (sooner in the case of Yugoslavia, which broke with the USSR in 1948, and later in the case of Albania) led to independence from Soviet domination. And a fourth group—consisting of the Baltic countries of Estonia, Latvia, and Lithuania, as well as the eastern part of

Romania that had been Bessarabia—found themselves absorbed into the USSR.

The one European country bordering the Soviet Union that escaped such a fate was Finland (despite having fought against the USSR). At the centre of postwar Finnish politics was the need to maintain good relations with the Soviet Union, with an accommodating foreign policy developed by Juho Kusti Paasikivi, the country's President from 1946 to 1956. In ceding territory to the USSR (finally agreed in the Paris Peace Treaty of 1947, and comprising roughly 11.5 per cent of Finland's prewar territory) and demonstrating that Finland would pose no threat to the Soviet Union, while drawing political parties from across the political spectrum into government, Finland was able to remain independent of the Soviet bloc and to maintain internal stability.

The transformation of the lands in what became the Soviet bloc into communist dictatorships began before the war ended, with the establishment of a Polish Committee of National Liberation in Lublin in opposition to the London Polish government-in-exile in July 1944, and continued through to the communist coup in Czechoslovakia in February 1948. The process followed a broadly similar pattern: initially, communists promoted collaboration with socialists and social democrats, as well as coalitions with non-socialist parties, in order to achieve what was described as a democratic political transformation; communists gained control of the security apparatus; socialist and communist parties were fused into a single party dominated by communists that, with the backing of their Soviet comrades, became the ruling parties of their respective states; political repression grew, as opponents of the transformation were prosecuted and imprisoned, while others retreated into private life or fled westwards; and by the spring of 1948 'people's democracies'—in effect, communist dictatorships that subordinated themselves to the USSR—were consolidated across eastern Europe. These events—particularly the coup in Czechoslovakia—shocked the West, causing left-wing parties in western Europe to distance themselves from Moscow, accelerating the development of a western military alliance, and cementing the Cold War division of postwar Europe.

With the creation of the 'people's democracies' the ruling communist parties in central and eastern Europe became mass organizations, integrating many people who at least passively had supported the previous, wartime regimes. In Poland the Polish Workers' Party grew from about 30,000 members at the beginning of 1945 to 10 times that number four months later; in December 1948, when it merged with the Polish Socialist Party, the resulting Polish United Workers' Party claimed a million members. In Hungary, the Communist Party grew from an underground organization with roughly 3,000 members in November 1944 to a party with 500,000 members (5.7 per cent of the country's population) in October 1945 and 887,000 members in 1948/9; and in Czechoslovakia the Communist Party grew from 27,000 to 1,788,000 members during the same period. Similarly, the membership of the Romanian Communist Party grew from that of an underground organization with a mere 5,000–6,000 members in October 1944 to roughly one million by 1947.

Postwar politics was not least a politics of revenge. Public rituals of retribution against alleged collaborators at the war's end—from shaving the heads of women who had had sexual relationships with German soldiers to the prosecution and execution of collaborators—were one aspect of this. The repressive politics of the regimes installed in eastern Europe in the late 1940s were another. The supposed need to root out real or imagined enemies was amplified by the split between Yugoslavia and the USSR in 1948, when Josip Broz Tito resisted Stalin's demands for subordination to the Soviet–Cominform line. Across Soviet-dominated eastern Europe campaigns were stoked against alleged 'Trotskyist, Titoist, Zionist, bourgeois-nationalist traitors'. Policing was politicized and radicalized; as Heinz Hoffmann, Vice-President of the (East) German Administration of the

Interior (and later GDR Minister for National Defence), asserted in September 1949 there was 'no separation between political and police work'. Hundreds of thousands of people were arrested and put in camps. In Czechoslovakia after the 1948 coup roughly a quarter of a million people were put on trial and interned, and three times that number were on the receiving end of economic and social sanctions; in Hungary roughly one-tenth of the entire population were arrested, prosecuted, imprisoned, or deported; and in Romania the number in prison, labour camps, or forced to work building the Danube–Black Sea Canal was more than a million.

Within months of Stalin's death in March 1953, however, there began a series of popular revolts against communist rule. The main protagonists were workers—the very group whose interests communist parties purported to represent. The protests were sparked by attempts to raise work norms and quotas; more generally, the revolts reflected anger about low living standards and lack of decent housing, and the contrast between the propaganda glorifying socialism and actual conditions. There had been unrest before March 1953—between 1948 and 1953 over 200 strikes had occurred in the main industrial regions of Czechoslovakia; and the Wismut uranium mines near Saalfeld in the GDR saw protests against dangerous working conditions. However, the post-Stalin protests and the threat they posed to the postwar pro-Soviet regimes were far more serious.

The first of these occurred in the western Czech city of Plzeň (Pilsen), the site of the Škoda Works, as economic and currency reforms that devalued people's savings along with increased work quotas were imposed at the end of May 1953. In response Škoda workers went on strike; crowds marched into the town centre and attacked the city hall, demands were raised for an end to one-party rule, and strikes broke out in other Czech cities, before the offending measures were rescinded and the unrest suppressed. A couple of weeks later a similar chain of events unfolded in the

GDR, where, faced with a deteriorating economic situation, the state had increased work norms. Under pressure from their Soviet comrades, the GDR leadership announced a 'New Course' that promised to abandon forced collectivization of agriculture and persecution of religious activity—but left the increased work norms in place. In response, on 16 June building workers in East Berlin downed tools on the Stalinallee (the GDR's showpiece reconstruction project) and marched on government ministries; on the following day protesters massed in front of the ministries, demanding free elections and in some cases the overthrow of the government. The unrest spread rapidly to industrial centres across the GDR, before the uprising was suppressed by Soviet forces stationed in the country.

The next eruption took place in Poland in late June 1956, when workers at the huge Cegielski factory in Poznań went on strike after the government raised work quotas. Workers from other factories joined in; crowds gathered in the Poznań city centre and the local party headquarters and office of the Ministry of Public Security were attacked. As in the GDR three years earlier, the unrest was put down quickly by the military—in this case the Polish military, but led by Soviet officers (Poland's Defence Minister at the time, Konstantin Rokossovsky, who took personal control of the situation, was a Soviet general)—with substantial loss of life and hundreds of arrests.

Postwar eastern Europe's most explosive uprising occurred in Hungary. In the wake of the thaw signalled by Khrushchev's 'Secret Speech' in February 1956 and the events in Poland in June, discontent with Hungary's political system spilled over in late October with student demonstrations in Budapest. Radical protest turned into armed resistance after the government proclaimed a state of emergency and called for Soviet forces to intervene; citizens organized popular militias and fought against secret police and Soviet troops; workers' councils formed and took over the running of factories. On 24 October the reform-minded Imre Nagy

(Prime Minister between 1953 and 1955) was called upon to head the government. Nagy called for a ceasefire, agreed to establish a multi-party system, and, on 1 November 1956, declared Hungary's neutrality and withdrawal from the Warsaw Pact. This effectively promised to restructure Europe's postwar order, and on 4 November Soviet forces intervened to suppress the new government and its supporters. A week later the Hungarian Revolution was over. Some 2,500 Hungarians and 700 Soviet soldiers lost their lives; a pro-Soviet government, headed by János Kádár (who remained in power for the next 32 years), was installed; roughly 35,000 people were arrested and 350 executed. (Nagy later was arrested and tried for treason; he was executed in June 1958.)

While the turbulence that shook these regimes revealed the underlying instability of the Stalinist system imposed after the Second World War, its suppression paved the way for something of a stabilization of the political order in eastern Europe. The crushing of the uprisings was followed not by a return to the *status quo ante*, but by a more regularized system of authoritarian rule: thus in Hungary Kádár came to preside over what was termed 'goulash communism' in 'the "happiest barrack" of the socialist camp'; and in Poland Władysław Gomułka, who had been General Secretary of the Polish Workers' Party and prominent advocate of a 'Polish Road to Socialism' after the war, but then soon was removed from power, could return and tread a political path somewhat less fixed in the Soviet mould. Nevertheless, the Stalinist interlude (and the suppression of the revolts against it) left a residue of fear that helped to underpin eastern European communist regimes for decades and thus lend an air of permanence to Europe's political division—something reinforced by the crushing of Alexander Dubček's attempt to create 'socialism with a human face' with the Czechoslovak 'Prague Spring' of 1968.

On the western side of the continent countries emerging from the war enjoyed rather greater room for manoeuvre, while their politics were also inspired by hopes and desires for new beginnings. Whereas political life in postwar eastern Europe was shaped substantially by the Soviet Union, in postwar western Europe political life was influenced powerfully by the USA, and by visions of what a 'New Europe' should become after the catastrophe of the Second World War. The idea of a united Europe was not new. However, with the defeat of Germany and the end of the war, the decline in the power of individual western European states, and American postwar support for the principle of European union, the ideal of a 'New Europe'—a European 'supranational association' (Robert Schuman)—seemed possible. This developed into a political programme and drew the support of leading centrist politicians—notably Robert Schuman (French Minister of Finance in 1946, Prime Minister in 1947-8, and Foreign Minister from 1948), Jean Monnet (instigator of what became the European Coal and Steel Community, the ECSC), Konrad Adenauer (first Chancellor of the Federal Republic of Germany), and Alcide De Gasperi (Prime Minister of Italy from 1945 to 1953), and supported by Winston Churchill (who had argued in a major speech in Zurich in September 1946 for a 'United States of Europe, or whatever name it might take')—during the early postwar years (Figure 5).

The 'New Europe' needed new Europeans, and the postwar years saw efforts to foster European consciousness particularly among younger generations in western Europe, who were to be educated to overcome the divisive nationalisms of previous generations. A new European consciousness was promoted by the European Youth Campaign, which was funded by the CIA and which encouraged pro-European attitudes through propaganda campaigns during the 1950s, and by the European Movement, which was established formally in October 1948. The European Movement acted as an organization lobbying for European integration, and it influenced the creation of the Council of Europe (founded in 1949) and through that the European Convention on Human Rights (which came into force in 1953).

5. The monument *Homage to the Founding Fathers of Europe* in front of Robert Schuman's house in Scy-Chazelles (from left to right: Alcide De Gasperi, Robert Schuman, Jean Monnet, Konrad Adenauer).

However, early postwar aspirations for a supra-national European organization were disappointed. Hopes that Britain would take a leading role in European unification were not realized, as the UK emphasized instead its security partnership and 'special relationship' with the USA; and the Council of Europe did not in fact become a vehicle for European integration. Opinion was split between those in continental western Europe who looked to a more integrated, federalist Europe—who formed the ECSC in 1951 and were the core of what subsequently became the European Economic Community (EEC)—and those who looked to looser, intergovernment cooperation, most notably in the UK—who were to form the European Free Trade Association in 1960. Efforts to achieve a common western European defence policy were overtaken by the establishment in 1949 of the North Atlantic Treaty Organization (NATO), with the USA its dominant member.

Initially it had been the political left that appeared to gain strength in western Europe. The rejection of those who had collaborated with occupation regimes, and the credit that left-wing parties gained through resistance to German occupation (at least during the second half of the war), boosted popular support for the left. This lifted left-wing parties into government: during 1945 and 1946 communists participated in coalition governments in Belgium, France, and Italy; and socialist or social-democratic governments in Scandinavia and the UK launched programmes of nationalization and extended the welfare state.

The early postwar resurgence of the left in western Europe was accompanied by a growth in labour organization. In Italy and (West) Germany, trade unions rapidly gained members after the destruction of the Fascist and National Socialist regimes. The German Trade Union Federation (*Deutscher Gewerkschaftsbund*, DGB) numbered two million members in the British Occupation Zone alone when it was established in April 1947, and when the trade unions merged into the DGB throughout the Federal Republic in October 1949 their membership was nearly five million. In Belgium, trade-union membership roughly doubled between 1945 and 1951. In France, the communist-influenced CGT (*Confédération Générale du Travail*—General Confederation of Labour) grew to a peak membership of more than 5.5 million members in 1946, and in 1947 and 1948 France saw the highest level of strike activity since the surge in labour militancy immediately after the First World War.

Nevertheless, success for the left proved short-lived, not least for western Europe's communist parties. In Italy, the Communist Party (PCI) benefited from its prominent role in the partisan campaign against German occupation after Mussolini's fall in July 1943 and attracted a mass membership after the war—rising to 1.7 million in 1945, 2.2 million in 1947, and 2.3 million in 1949—and mass electoral support—with nearly 19.0 per cent of the vote in the election for the Constituent Assembly in 1946 and 22.7 per cent in 1953. However, postwar Italian politics was anti-fascist across the board, and the PCI's electoral following lagged behind that of both Christian Democracy, which won 35.2 per cent of the vote in 1946, and the Italian Socialist Party (PSI), which secured 20.7 per cent. Communist success at the polls proved insufficient to achieve political power: from May 1947 the PCI was excluded from government by the Christian Democrat Prime Minister Alcide De Gasperi (under pressure from the United States) and, while becoming Italy's second most popular party, it remained in opposition at national level.

Like its Italian counterpart, the French Communist Party (*Parti communiste français*, PCF) built on its participation in the wartime *résistance*, as '*le parti des fusillés*' (the party of the executed). In the wake of the liberation it gathered support, attracting roughly 800,000 members for a short period and gaining 26.0 per cent of the vote in the elections of July 1946 and 28.2 per cent in November 1946. However, after participating in government between 1945 and 1947 it became something of a 'political pariah', as a result of France's governmental crisis of May 1947 and the street unrest supported by the PCF, and subsequently was consigned to opposition, until 1981. In Belgium too the Communist Party (*Kommunistische Partij van België*–KPB; *Parti communiste belge*–PCB) achieved postwar electoral success and participated in a government coalition with the socialists and the liberals from 1946 to 1947, but was removed from government in March 1947 when the socialist (and committed protagonist for European integration) Paul-Henri Spaak became Prime Minister.

It was the more conservative politicians—de Gaulle in France, Adenauer in West Germany, De Gasperi in Italy—who achieved the more lasting success. Where left-wing politicians were successful in western Europe—Clement Attlee and Ernest Bevin of the Labour Party in the UK, Paul-Henri Spaak in Belgium, and Einar Gerhardsen of the Labour Party in Norway—this was paralleled by their rejection of communism and commitment to the emerging western military alliance led by the USA.

Central to the political order of postwar Europe was Germany, and a key motive for postwar western European integration would be to overcome the long-standing enmity between France and Germany. Germany's sovereignty had been abolished with the country's defeat in 1945, and its fate then lay with the occupying powers. The Potsdam Agreement had stipulated that, 'so far as is practicable, there shall be uniformity of treatment of the German population throughout Germany'. However, this principle very quickly proved illusory, as the postwar political and economic demarcation on the European continent emerged through occupied Germany. The result was two rival postwar German states, both born in the autumn of 1949, when the three western occupation zones became the FRG and the Soviet Occupation Zone became the GDR.

In the west it was the Christian Democratic Union (CDU) under the leadership of Konrad Adenauer and the Social Democratic Party of Germany led by Kurt Schumacher that attracted most popular support. Their political success rested in large measure on identification with the west and rejection of the communist alternative, and both turned away from collaboration with their party comrades in the Soviet Zone. The modest regional electoral successes achieved by the revived Communist Party of Germany (*Kommunistische Partei Deutschlands*—KPD) during 1946 and 1947 proved temporary, and after the federal elections of September 1953 it no longer achieved representation in the country's parliament. (The KPD was banned in the Federal Republic in 1956. This was the second such prohibition in the FRG: in 1952, the neo-Nazi *Sozialistische Reichspartei* was banned.)

In the Soviet Occupation Zone (*Sowjetische Besatzungszone*—SBZ), however, political developments followed the pattern seen elsewhere within the Soviet orbit. There the KPD, supported by the Soviet occupation authorities, merged with the SPD in April 1946 to form the Socialist Unity Party of Germany (*Sozialistische*

Einheitspartei Deutschlands—SED), and then achieved success at the polls: in regional elections across the SBZ in October 1946, the SED received nearly half the vote (47.5 per cent). Subsequently, as occurred throughout the Soviet bloc, a communist-dominated 'unity' party of the left became the ruling party of a socialist state.

Although having been incorporated into the German Reich in 1938, and although it (like Germany) was divided into four occupation zones, Austria remained under joint occupation until granted full independence in May 1955, with a commitment to remain neutral. The Austrian Social Democrats, who re-christened their party the Socialist Party of Austria in 1945 (to be renamed again in 1991 as the Social Democratic Party of Austria), gained 44.6 per cent of the vote for the National Council (*Nationalrat*) in November 1945, after which they participated in coalition government; they largely maintained their popular backing (and almost uninterrupted participation in government) until the 1990s. By contrast, Austria's communists failed to win broad backing, gaining a mere 5.4 per cent of the vote in 1945; they participated in coalition government between 1945 and 1947, but subsequently lost support, and from 1959 no longer achieved representation in the *Nationalrat*.

There were, of course, the European countries that had neither fought nor been occupied during the Second World War. In some cases—Ireland, Sweden, and Switzerland—liberal democratic systems were able to continue largely uninterrupted. In Sweden, where the Social Democratic Labour Party had been in power continuously since 1932 (and continued so until 1976), the postwar trajectory was a matter more of developing the welfare state than achieving a political transformation. Neutral Switzerland and Ireland also emerged in the postwar period with their democratic political institutions intact.

The Iberian peninsula, however, saw the continuation of repressive dictatorship. For the Franco regime in Spain, which had emerged from its own (civil) war and was excluded from participation in the Marshall Plan in 1947, postwar transition meant moving from the outward dominance of the Falangist movement during the Second World War to what historian Paul Preston has described as 'the period of dour Christian Democrat rule between 1946 and 1957'. It also meant moving from the friendly wartime relations with the Axis powers to friendly postwar relations with the USA—to the point where, in September 1953, Spain signed a defence pact with the USA. In Portugal, where the autocratic *Estado Novo* ('New State') regime of António de Oliveira Salazar had aligned more with the western powers during the Second World War and maintained itself in the postwar years, there was less need to reorient external policies to new realities, and it was among the founding members of NATO in 1949.

The men who dominated European politics during the early postwar years were shaped by their experiences before and during the Second World War. The leaders who emerged in eastern Europe had dedicated themselves to the communist movement and anti-Fascist struggle and had spent the war either in the USSR or in resistance movements in their own countries. In the western half of the continent leading politicians also carried their wartime experiences into postwar politics. Charles de Gaulle, who had refused to accept France's military defeat in 1940 and escaped to England to lead the Free French Forces, was the head of the Provisional Government of the French Republic from June 1944 until he resigned in 1946, but returned to power in 1958 and dominated French politics as President of the (Fifth) Republic from 1959 to 1969. On the other side of the Rhine, the veteran Catholic politician Konrad Adenauer, who would be (West) German Chancellor from 1949 to 1963, had been dismissed as mayor of Cologne in April 1933 and spent the Nazi years as a pensioner out of the public eye (with short periods of imprisonment). Alcide De Gasperi, the Christian Democrat leader of eight Italian governments between 1945 and 1953, had opposed fascism and been under police surveillance and imprisoned during the 1920s and subsequently spent most of the period of Fascist rule working as a cataloguer in the Vatican Library.

By the early 1950s, new political systems were in place on both sides of the east–west divide. On the one hand, this development may be seen as the construction and hardening of the front line of the Cold War, as much of the world was divided into two hostile political, military, and economic blocs. On the other, this may be regarded as two contrasting responses to the challenge of building a political and economic order after the shattering experiences of the Second World War.

The political orders established in Europe after the Second World War dealt with the destructive and painful legacies of that war in another sense as well: by putting the uncomfortable histories of the war years behind and replacing them with myth. In both east and west, they portrayed themselves as free of blame for the horrors of the war years, and as heirs to democratic or to socialist traditions that supposedly had little or nothing to do with the violence and crimes of the wartime regimes and their populations. For Germany, where the issue was more difficult to dismiss, neither the FRG nor the GDR regarded themselves as the heir to the 'Third Reich'; and in Austria a national consciousness arose which distanced itself from Germany.

The peoples of postwar Europe had to clear away not only the physical rubble with which they were confronted, but also the mental and spiritual rubble, and they accomplished this task in part through a collective, public amnesia. The division of Europe made that easier, lending selective public amnesia an importance in justifying political confrontation, romanticizing some elements of recent history and demonizing others. The result was what historian Dan Stone describes as 'the rise of the postwar consensus': 'consensus enforced' in socialist authoritarian eastern Europe and 'consensus of silence' in the capitalist pluralist west.

Chapter 5
Building new societies

After the Second World War Europe faced massive social and economic dislocation. In most combatant countries—the UK was a significant exception—economic activity in 1945 was a fraction of what it had been on the eve of the conflict. Tens of millions of undernourished Europeans had to be fed, and tens of millions of homeless Europeans had to be housed—challenges made all the greater by the destruction of industrial and agricultural infrastructure, the return of millions of soldiers, and the massive loss of life (particularly of young men) that left families hollowed out and population structures profoundly skewed.

At the same time, enormous challenges presented enormous opportunities. On both sides of the east–west divide that emerged in postwar Europe, states aimed to rebuild and restructure societies: new housing both to remedy the acute shortages that arose from wartime destruction and to replace the inadequate and unhealthy dwellings that had housed millions of Europeans before the war, new and enhanced social-welfare systems to provide comprehensive social security, and new and expanded educational institutions to offer more people opportunities that previously had been reserved to a privileged minority.

The recent conflict had demonstrated how the state could be expanded to fight a war, and many now believed that an expanded state could serve the needs of postwar society. Alongside visions of a brave new world were memories of what had occurred after 1918, when economic dislocation, unemployment, and conflict plagued the European continent. Across Europe there was widespread conviction that what had occurred after the First World War must not be repeated after the Second. 'Never Again' was the rallying cry.

For millions of Europeans after the war, the immediate challenge was to find somewhere to live. In France it had been estimated on the eve of the conflict that 1.5 million new dwellings were required to achieve equilibrium in the housing market, and that was before nearly two million dwellings were destroyed during the war; in Britain, the war left a million homes either destroyed or desperately requiring repair. Yet as great as was the challenge to provide adequate housing in western Europe, in eastern Europe it was even greater. In Poland's 'recovered territories', Polish settlers were greeted by scenes of utter destruction: Wiesław Sauter, who had been charged by the new Polish administration with setting up school systems along the Oder in western Poland, described one town when he had arrived in October 1945 as looking 'scarcely better than Rome burned down by Nero'. In Russia, the city of Smolensk lost roughly 88 per cent of its housing due to the fighting, Voronezh 83 per cent, and Rostov-on-Don three-quarters; in Leningrad somewhere between 500,000 and a million people had been made homeless. In the Soviet Union as a whole, in 1945 the urban housing stock was approximately one-quarter less than it had been in 1940. The living quarters remaining available to millions of Europeans in the early postwar years were small, heated poorly if at all, often without running water or decent sanitary facilities, and providing an ideal environment for the spread of tuberculosis.

In 1948 Hans Berlage, the postwar head of the Hamburg City Planning Office, wrote that 'before the war a thorough renewal of the city seemed a hopeless wish of the city planner', but wartime destruction made such urban renewal possible. One observer in bomb-scarred Coventry asserted: 'The Jerries cleaned out the core of the city, a chaotic mess, and now we can start anew.' In London the architect-planner Sir Patrick Abercrombie and the architect J. H. Forshaw had already published the County of London Plan in 1943, proposing how a new London would be built from the ruins of the old; in response the postwar Labour government passed the New Towns Act of 1946, creating a wave of planned new towns which in the London area alone were to house more than a million people by the end of the century. Similarly, in heavily bombed Rotterdam the Outline Plan of 1946 for its reconstruction reflected a broad conviction that the wartime damage offered an occasion to renew and modernize the city. Wartime destruction had created what the German architectural journalist-critic and modernist architect Alfons Leitl described in 1946 as a unique opportunity to effect not 'small laborious corrections', but rather 'a fundamental reorganization' of the environment (Figure 6).

6. A typical combined shop and dwelling block in Groenendaal, completed in 1946, in the centre of Rotterdam's war-devastated area.

The determination to effect a 'fundamental reorganization' was particularly strong in the eastern half of the continent, where it was driven by a political vision and where the urban environment was transformed after 1945. There the transformation had three main aspects: the rebuilding and development of existing cities, most notably the capital cities in the Soviet bloc (Warsaw, Bucharest, Sofia, Prague, Budapest, Minsk); the urbanization and industrialization of smaller cities in what had been largely rural regions (e.g. Olsztyn—formerly Allenstein—in north-eastern Poland and Schwedt in the north-east of the GDR); and the creation of new, planned socialist industrial cities built on green-field sites to service giant new heavy-industrial combines: Nowa Huta (New Foundry) near Cracow in Poland, Stalinstadt (Stalin City, renamed Eisenhüttenstadt in 1961) in the GDR (Figure 7), Dunapentele (named Sztálinváros (Stalin City) in 1951 and renamed Dunaújváros (Danube New City) in 1961) in Hungary.

Societies across the European continent were transformed as a result of a phenomenal postwar expansion of industrial economies.

7. A street with residential blocks in Stalinstadt.

In the west, major beneficiaries of the 30 years of unprecedented economic growth that followed the Second World War were Italy and Germany. Italy saw a postwar 'economic miracle' that transformed it from a relatively poor and largely agricultural country into a major industrial power. West Germany's 'economic miracle' manifested itself not just in established industrial regions such as the Ruhr, but also in Bavaria, where the proportion of the employed population working in agriculture declined from 37.7 per cent in 1939 to 21.6 per cent in 1961 and 13.2 per cent in 1970. To the east, where postwar communist regimes were determined to press ahead with industrialization at breakneck speed, the transformation was even more remarkable. In Poland, for example, in 1970 the urban population outnumbered their rural cousins for the first time.

Postwar European societies were also transformed by a remarkable expansion of state-run social welfare. European governments committed themselves to developing and extending the welfare state. Increasingly it was accepted that welfare provision should be universal—that is, with a right to receive benefits on the basis of citizenship—and should encompass not just social insurance (i.e. against unemployment or accident), but also social assistance and social services. (Thus the 1946 Constitution of the French Fourth Republic committed the 'Nation' to 'guarantee to all, notably to children, mothers and elderly workers, protection of their health, material security, rest and leisure', and stipulated that 'all people who, by virtue of their age, physical or mental condition, or economic situation, are incapable of working, shall have the right to receive suitable means of existence from society'.)

In the immediate aftermath of the war most European countries had not been in a position to finance expansive social programmes, but the economic boom of the 1950s and 1960s created the basis for a huge growth in the state provision of welfare in western Europe. While Britain's Labour government (1945–51) had constructed a welfare state that supported its citizens 'from cradle to grave' during the years of postwar austerity, elsewhere the development of a comprehensive welfare state came somewhat later. Even in Sweden, which had remained neutral during the war and where the development of the welfare state had begun earlier, it did not come fully into fruition until the late 1950s. What followed was 'the golden age of welfare state expansion' and increasing state intervention in economic and social affairs. As the Social Democratic Party and the National Federation of Trade Unions in Sweden asserted in 1971, 'we have the means to be generous toward those who aren't successful in our complicated society'. The proportion of public expenditure devoted to social welfare, in particular to old-age pensions, grew (Table 1). The result was described as 'the happy conjuncture ... of high economic growth and responsiveness to social and economic needs'.

This growth in social expenditure occurred as gross domestic product itself was increasing in absolute terms: that is to say, social expenditure comprised a rapidly growing proportion of rapidly growing economies. In the UK, between 1949/50 and 1972/3 social spending by central government grew by two and a half times; its share of central government expenditure grew from 20.7 per cent

Table 1. Proportion of GDP devoted to social expenditure, 1960–75 (%)

	1960	1975
France	14.4	26.3
West Germany	17.1	27.8
Italy	13.7	20.6
Netherlands	12.8	29.3
Sweden	15.6	27.4
United Kingdom	12.4	19.6

to 28.1 per cent (while the share of spending on defence fell by roughly a third, to 16.9 per cent); between 1960 and 1972, UK GDP increased by a bit over one-third, but social spending nearly doubled. In France, whereas pensions had constituted 3.6 per cent of the central government budget in 1953 they comprised 6.5 per cent in 1972 (while the share of military expenditures fell in the same period from 16.9 to 9.0 per cent). In West Germany spending on social welfare programmes increased from 12.3 billion DM in 1950 to 228.7 billion in 1972 (in current prices), while its share of GDP grew from 12.6 per cent to 27.8 per cent in the same period; in real terms spending on pensions was eight times as much in 1972 as in 1950.

The 1950s and 1960s were a period of welfare optimism. In 2003 Walter Korpi (of the Swedish Institute of Social Research, University of Stockholm) observed: 'Once upon a time—not that long ago—there was consensus in Western Europe that the welfare states' full employment and expanding social-citizenship rights inaugurated after the end of World War II had come to stay.' Then the welfare state hit the buffers. The economic crisis of the 1970s, with its combination of high inflation, sluggish economic growth, and the end of full employment, effectively put an end to the 'golden age' of welfare-state expansion. During the 1980s and 1990s governments began to restructure and to some extent even dismantle the welfare state: this was characterized by the privatization of welfare services, restrictions on entitlements and more restrictive conditions for qualifying for benefits, a shift towards targeting and means-testing, and limited increases or cuts in the real cash value of benefits. The optimism of the earlier postwar decades evaporated.

In eastern Europe social expenditure also rose substantially after the war, as socialist regimes took an extremely interventionist approach to social as well as economic policy. However, while the proportions of GDP devoted to social welfare in eastern Europe, before the stagnation and decline of the 1970s and 1980s, had been comparable to those in western Europe, the practice differed in two important respects. First, it proceeded from a lower base, as postwar eastern Europe generally was poorer and less industrial and had suffered greater material and human losses during the war. Second, there was less emphasis on financial redistribution and more on free or heavily subsidized provision. Pensions may have been meagre in cash terms, but health care, child care, public transportation, and housing were incredibly cheap or free. Rents cost a pittance (although it was often difficult to gain access to a dwelling); child care often was provided by the state (not least to enable women with small children to work outside the home); and many items of everyday expenditure, in particular basic foodstuffs, were heavily subsidized.

A problem that plagued the socialist regimes of the Soviet bloc throughout the postwar years was that compared with the capitalist west, which achieved greater prosperity and thus greater social welfare, these regimes were found wanting. After initially aiming to build planned industrial economies (often at the expense of consumer-goods production), during the 1970s a number of eastern European states turned towards devoting more resources to social welfare and consumption. In the GDR Erich Honecker proclaimed the 'unity of economic and social policy', and in the wake of the protests of December 1970 in Poland Edward Gierek aimed to improve the availability of consumer goods and services, provide better housing, and looked forward to a shorter working week. Welfare was to be the basis of a social contract that would underpin socialist rule as it moved to one based more on consumption. However, the resources needed for this transformation were limited and, as discontent in Poland during the 1970s demonstrated, making Sunkist lemons and Pepsi Cola available to consumers was not sufficient to buy social peace. In eastern Europe too the expansion of the welfare state would hit the buffers.

Central to the development of postwar welfare policies was the position of women. Millions had lost partners and breadwinners during the war, and subsequently had to take up paid employment while simultaneously bringing up children. Consequently many needed state aid and became what has been described as being 'wedded to welfare'. The pressures were particularly great in eastern Europe, where wartime losses had been so high and where communist regimes aimed to construct industrial economies, which necessitated drawing women into paid employment (alongside concern about the birth rate). Welfare policies designed to increase the labour force by enabling women to work outside the home included expanded maternity benefits and extended work leave for mothers, as well as the provision of institutionalized child care. However, notwithstanding policies designed to draw women into the labour force in eastern Europe and rising levels of women's paid employment in western Europe, the assumptions underlying the postwar extension of the welfare state essentially rested on the model of households consisting of a married male worker and dependent family.

New postwar households needed new postwar housing, and from the 1950s onwards, Europe's housing stock was transformed. In the FRG, between the currency reform in June 1948 and the autumn of 1952, 1.2 million social-housing units were built, providing homes for some five million people (roughly 10 per cent of the entire population). In Italy, between 1951 and 1961 the number of dwellings was increased by nearly a quarter (23.3 per cent) while the population of the country grew by 6.2 per cent; during the same period the number of people per dwelling decreased by 13.8 per cent and the number of people per room by 15 per cent. In France, from the 1950s onwards the government supported the construction of vast numbers of rent-controlled dwellings, the HLM (*habitations à loyer modéré*), which came to house a sixth of the entire French population. In Britain, during the period of the postwar Labour government (1945–51) nearly one million units were constructed, largely as local-government council housing; by 1957 roughly 2.5 million houses and flats had been built.

Housing developments sprang up on the outskirts of existing cities, in what has been described for France as *une nouvelle organisation de l'espace*. Inspired by the example of the British New Towns, French planners embarked during the 1960s on an ambitious programme of creating new towns on the outskirts of Paris; within 20 years they had roughly five million inhabitants, considerably outnumbering the population of Paris within the boundaries of the old city. Beyond the Paris region new mass housing developments were built as well—such as Planoise on the western outskirts of the provincial city of Besançon, the construction of which began in 1962 and which grew to become the most populous district of the city. In West Berlin during the 1960s and early 1970s the huge new settlement Gropiusstadt (named for its architect Walter Gropius after his death) was created in the south-eastern corner of the city, eventually containing 18,500 dwellings (mostly social housing) in high-rise blocks; and in the north of the city (along the Wall) another huge high-rise project, the Märkisches Viertel (with 17,000 units), was built. During the late 1960s and early 1970s Sweden embarked on its hugely ambitious '*Miljonprogrammet*' (Million Programme) to build a million new dwellings in a country of only eight million inhabitants. These massive housing programmes formed an important element of Europe's postwar urbanization and changed the character of many cities. The societies of postwar Europe were increasingly urban societies.

The postwar housing boom changed not only where, but also how people lived. Across western Europe new dwellings were constructed not simply to ameliorate shortages and offer homes for people migrating into urban areas, but also to provide their inhabitants with modern amenities. Describing the new domestic environment in Britain, the social scientist Mark Abrams noted in 1959 that 'for the first time in modern British history the working-class home, as well as the middle-class home, has become a place that is warm, comfortable, and able to provide its own fireside entertainment—in fact, pleasant to live in'. The trend towards smaller families and away from multi-generation households combined with postwar housing schemes and a new aspiration to re-engineer the private spaces and lives of citizens, to make space available for the enjoyment of private lives. As a tenant in the Grindel high-rises in Hamburg, built in the early postwar years, later recalled, the best thing was 'that one had a toilet and a stove of one's own, that I could cook when I wanted'.

Not only in the west but in eastern Europe too huge numbers of dwellings were built in the postwar years. From Nová Ostrava in Czechoslovakia to Nowa Huta in southern Poland, from high-rise housing on the outskirts of Riga in Latvia to Stalinstadt in the GDR, across socialist eastern Europe hundreds of thousands of new housing units were built. In Poland over three million were constructed between the end of the war and the late 1970s. Although building standards were often rather poor and although these dwellings would often be considered undesirable after the collapse of eastern European socialism, they were a distinct improvement on the housing that they replaced—offering their tenants indoor plumbing, central heating, and private space often for the first time in their lives.

The lives of many Europeans were also transformed by the broadening of educational provision. When the Second World War ended, in many European countries the most common school-leaving age (and thus the level of educational attainment) was between the ages of 12 and 14, and even this was often weakly enforced. Only a minority, coming from the middle and upper classes, had a secondary education—fewer than one in 20 of Italy's postwar population had completed secondary school—and only a tiny fraction of Europeans, almost exclusively from the upper and upper-middle classes, had gone on to university. In 1949 there were just over 130,000 university students in France, fewer than 100,000 in the UK, only 50,000 in Spain, and just 15,000 in Sweden.

In subsequent decades this changed dramatically, as university education was opened up to strata well beyond the traditional elites. By 1960, the number of university students in Britain, France, and Italy was already roughly three times what it had been on the eve of the Second World War. The number of students enrolled at universities in the FRG rose from 128,528 in 1950 to 246,939 in 1960 and 421,976 in 1970. In the UK, the number of universities grew from 17 at the end of the Second World War to 26 in 1960 and 47 in 1969. In France the number of university students increased by two and a half times between 1960 and 1968, from 200,000 to half a million. Not only did the total numbers of students rise, but the proportion of women rose even faster: between 1950 and 1975 the proportion of female students in colleges and universities in western Europe nearly doubled, from 22 per cent to 39 per cent. This expansion opened new cultural and economic horizons to hundreds of thousands of Europeans—and also created the context for the student unrest of the late 1960s, notably in new postwar universities (e.g. the Free University in West Berlin, the University of Essex in England, and—most famously—the Université Paris Nanterre).

In socialist eastern Europe too the university system expanded substantially. In Yugoslavia, 14 new universities opened between 1957 and 1979 (before the war there had been only three, and two more opened in 1949); student enrolment in Yugoslav universities, which had been tiny in the early postwar years, rose from 140,574 in 1960 to 261,203 in 1970 and 394,992 in 1975. In Poland the number of students in higher education grew from 94,785 in 1947–8 to 251,864 in 1965–6; in Hungary there were six times as many students in higher education in 1962–3 as there had been in 1937–8; and in Romania the number of students increased fivefold between 1938 and 1966. The proportion of women attending university in eastern Europe was even higher than in the west, increasing from 34 per cent to 48 per cent between 1950 and 1975. And whereas during the first two postwar decades university education in western Europe remained limited largely to the children of the upper-middle and upper classes, in eastern Europe communist governments aimed to extend it to the working class and the rural population. During the early postwar years preference in admission was given to children of workers and peasants: 'Workers and Peasants' Faculties' were created in order to break the 'cultural monopoly of the bourgeoisie' and to bring into the universities new classes of people who would provide politically reliable cadres for the postwar communist regimes.

The expansion of higher education meant that the populations of both eastern and western Europe became markedly better educated. Its beneficiaries were Europeans who came of age during the 1960s and 1970s. Consequently Europe's postwar generations gained perspectives and expectations that set them apart from their parents, who had experienced war as adults. Also, increasingly they met their marriage partners at university rather than in the towns and villages where they had grown up.

Postwar societies were built in large measure by postwar families. Europe's population grew by roughly 30 per cent between 1940 and the early 1970s, despite wartime losses and emigration during the early postwar years. In part the population growth was due to improvements in public health and declines in mortality, a good measure of which was the steep decline in deaths due to tuberculosis in every European country between 1950 and 1971. However, it was also due to two interrelated developments that shaped family life in the aftermath of the war: a postwar marriage boom and a postwar baby boom.

The return of millions of men from military service and prisoner-of-war camps, as well as the return of both men and women from places of forced labour, led to a surge in marriages across much of the continent. This postwar 'peak in nuptiality' was partly a consequence of delayed marriages contracted soon after the end of the war, making the years immediately after 1945 a period in which marriage was very attractive. After the war the proportion of women who married increased almost everywhere in Europe—except among middle-aged women in some countries in eastern Europe

(Bulgaria, Greece, Yugoslavia, Hungary, Poland) where marriage rates had already been very high—and the proportion of young women (i.e. those between 20 and 24) who were married increased sharply.

The surge in marriages was followed by a surge in births, but not uniformly across the continent. In occupied Germany the baby boom was delayed due to war casualties and the slow return of the millions of men from prisoner-of-war camps; and some countries (e.g. Portugal, Spain, Italy, Hungary, Greece, Bulgaria) saw no noticeable postwar spurt in births. Nevertheless, much of Europe saw an increase in the numbers of children born during the first two postwar decades.

However, from the middle of the 1960s marriage rates began to decline across Europe and the age at which people married began to increase. The postwar baby boom proved a temporary exception to a long-term decline in birth rates that stretched from the 19th century to the 20th. From the 1960s that decline resumed with a 'baby bust', a consequence of which in many European countries was an increasingly ageing population towards the end of the 20th century.

With the establishment of millions of new families and a temporary rise in births, the postwar decades saw the zenith of the nuclear family. This, in turn, helped to shape the political and cultural climate. Socially conservative political parties that put supposedly traditional family values at the centre of their appeal and social policies, in particular Christian Democrat parties, were strikingly successful in western Europe, and postwar welfare states regarded the (nuclear) family as the cornerstone of a healthy society.

The postwar baby boom led to a substantial increase in the number of adolescents in Europe during the late 1950s and the 1960s, and they comprised a particularly large proportion of the population in many European countries. In Germany in 1965 the largest birth cohort was of those aged between 25 and 29; in France in 1970 the largest birth cohorts were of those aged 24 and under; in both Denmark and Sweden in 1970 the largest birth cohort was of those aged between 20 and 24. These cohorts grew up in the increasing prosperity of the postwar years, spent longer in school than their parents had done, had increasing access to higher education, could use new methods of contraception, and benefited from generally buoyant employment possibilities. This was the generation whose members joined the rebellions of the 1960s, from the streets of Paris, London, and West Berlin in western Europe to Prague and Belgrade in the east of the continent. In 1968 the children of postwar Europe had come of age.

Postwar European societies contained not only large numbers of adolescents and young adults, but also millions of men who had experienced military service and war—men who then established postwar families and became the fathers of postwar children, who came to occupy leadership positions in politics and the economy, who formed a major slice of postwar electorates, and who became teachers in the educational institutions that expanded after the Second World War.

In countries that had emerged from the war on the victorious side, many veterans would look back on their military service with pride. Soviet veterans who had survived their 'Great Patriotic War'—of the just under 34.5 million people who served in the Soviet armed forces during the Second World War, 25.3 million had survived in 1945—were feted in public and brought into schools to speak of their exploits and inspire younger generations; British veterans could relish their association with their country's 'finest hour'; French *résistants* would celebrate their participation in a heroic resistance struggle against German occupation. Associations of veterans attracted mass memberships. In Britain, the membership of the Royal British Legion grew to three million at its peak in 1950. Even in West Germany, while the majority of former

Wehrmacht soldiers did not join veterans' groups, a sizeable minority did.

Postwar Europe was also hardly devoid of active soldiers, as it became the front line of the Cold War. While the USSR maintained large forces in central and eastern Europe in the wake of the Second World War—in 1946 roughly 700,000 Soviet occupation troops were in Germany alone—western military presence was not insubstantial. In 1947–8 the UK had 140,000 troops in Germany and Austria, the USA had 126,000, France 80,000, Belgium 24,000, Norway 4,400, and Denmark 4,000. When one adds the home armies of France (270,000), the Netherlands (108,000), Belgium (50,000), and Denmark (22,000), the total on the continent was over 800,000. (The US military presence grew rapidly in the early 1950s; by the end of 1952 the number of American military personnel in western Europe exceeded 400,000.)

During the 1950s and 1960s most European states maintained conscription and substantial military forces, whether as members of the NATO and Warsaw Pact military alliances or to fight against anti-colonial insurgencies. In 1957, when the UK Defence Minister Duncan Sandys called for an end to conscription, the strength of the British Army stood at some 373,000; the West German Bundeswehr, which inducted its first soldiers at the beginning of 1956, numbered over 400,000 personnel by the mid-1960s and at the end of the 1960s neared its planned strength of a half a million. On the other side of the east–west divide, the Polish government reintroduced conscription and built up its army to an establishment of 400,000 men, the second largest army (after that of the USSR) in the Warsaw Pact.

Not surprisingly, fear of war was widespread in postwar Europe. War was very close to Europeans—both as recent lived experience and as threat associated with the Cold War. Nowhere was this more apparent than in postwar Germany: in West Germany three-quarters of the respondents in an opinion poll in January 1950 stated their opposition to themselves, their sons, or their husbands becoming soldiers. Similar sentiments surfaced on the other side of the German–German border, where in the summer of 1952 the police noted popular alarm at the creation of the 'People's Police in Barracks' (the forerunner of the GDR's National People's Army). Another expression of the fear of war was the Campaign for Nuclear Disarmament, which was founded in London in 1957 and organized prominent but ultimately unsuccessful campaigns against Britain's nuclear weapons and, later, the stationing of American nuclear weapons in the UK.

War left its stamp especially on the millions of Europeans who had been subjected to forced migration: Poles from what had been eastern Poland; Germans from the former eastern Prussian provinces, the Sudetenland, and other areas of German settlement in eastern and southern Europe; Hungarians transferred from Czechoslovakia to Hungary; Finns forced to leave Karelia after the Soviet–Finnish War in 1940, returned during the 'Continuation War' of 1941–4, and subsequently evacuated anew from what again was in the USSR. To these were added Europeans removed from former colonies: Italians forced to leave Albania and Fascist Italy's African colonies after the Second World War; French *pieds noirs* who fled Algeria upon its independence in the early 1960s; Portuguese *retornados* who fled Angola and Mozambique upon their independence in the mid-1970s.

The early postwar years also saw substantial European *emigration*. Many Europeans, viewing landscapes of wartime destruction, housing shortages, low living standards, and high unemployment, chose to leave, often for the new world. In the Netherlands, postwar governments (regarding the country, which had to accept 300,000 post-colonial migrants from the former Dutch East Indies, to be overpopulated) actively promoted emigration; half a million Dutch emigrated at this time, a third of whom eventually returned. From 1950 to 1960 roughly 800,000 Germans left for countries overseas (three-quarters to the USA). Even greater numbers left the UK, seeking a new life in particular in Australia, New Zealand, South Africa, Canada, and the USA: it has been estimated that between 1950 and 1998 roughly 7.3 million people left the UK for non-European destinations. And European Jews who had survived wartime mass murder campaigns and faced continued hostility in Europe often sought to leave as soon as they could, mostly for Palestine/Israel or the USA; in the summer of 1946 alone between 90,000 and 95,000 Jewish survivors from eastern Europe, Germany, Austria, or Italy reached Palestine illegally on ships.

The next chapter of postwar European migration consisted of the movement of migrants into western European countries in search of employment and better living standards: Italians to postwar Britain, France, Switzerland, and West Germany, Portuguese to France (and to Jersey!), Yugoslavs to Germany. At the same time, western European countries began to see increasing migration of people from colonies and erstwhile colonies—North Africans into France, Indonesians into the Netherlands, South Asians and West Indians into Britain.

In this regard postwar eastern Europe diverged from the west. Ideological commitments to internationalism notwithstanding, after the immediate postwar period (when frontiers still were porous) the socialist states of eastern Europe largely restricted migration. The initial exception was the GDR, which sealed its border with the FRG in 1952, but not to West Berlin until the building of the Berlin Wall in August 1961; consequently, between the establishment of the GDR in 1949 and the construction of the Wall roughly 3.8 million GDR citizens left for West Germany (while some 400,000 Germans moved in the opposite direction). Some smaller waves of emigration from eastern Europe took place following political upheaval: in 1956–7 roughly 194,000 Hungarians left their country following the defeat of the Hungarian Revolution, before the border between Hungary and

Austria was effectively closed to migration; in 1968–9 about 190,000 people fled Czechoslovakia during the 'Prague Spring' and after its suppression; and in 1980–1 an estimated quarter of a million Poles left for western Europe following the imposition of martial law. However, as long as the regimes of socialist eastern Europe remained stable, their borders remained closed to mass migration.

Underlying so many of the transformations that shaped European societies during the postwar decades was the combination of generational shift and economic growth. This was also apparent in countries that had avoided direct military involvement in the Second World War. War had not smashed social structures in Sweden, Switzerland, Portugal, or Ireland. Nevertheless, many of the transformations experienced by their populations after 1945 paralleled those experienced by people living in countries that had fought or been fought over during the Second World War. The declines in the proportion of people employed in agriculture in Spain and Portugal between 1950 and 1980 were not very different from the declines in Finland and Greece; a comprehensive expansion of the welfare state occurred both in Britain, which had been at war from 1939 to 1945, and in Sweden, which had remained neutral during the conflict.

While not all the social transformations that unfolded in postwar Europe may have been direct consequences of war, societies in both former combatant countries and those that avoided direct military involvement in the Second World War were affected by common political, economic, and social transformations that followed the conflict. The immense challenges left by war created much of the foundation on which millions of Europeans would construct new societies in its wake.

Chapter 6
From scarcity to plenty

Postwar Europe saw one of the most remarkable economic transformations in modern history. When the Second World War ended, Europeans faced overwhelming economic problems: the destruction of industrial and transport infrastructure; unemployment following the winding-down of war production and the demobilization of huge numbers of soldiers; inflation, as a consequence of massive wartime deficit spending; lack of foreign exchange needed to pay for imports; terrible housing shortages; demographic distortions, with the deaths of millions of young men; widespread malnutrition; and vast numbers of people uprooted. Even by 1950, when much of Europe had returned to the *status quo ante* in terms of economic activity, the continent was hardly prosperous. The thought that within two decades war-torn Europe—at least its western half—could experience an unprecedented economic boom and emerge into an 'Age of Affluence' (Tony Judt), would have seemed unbelievable.

Yet in the three decades from 1945 Europe's economy grew faster than at any other time in its history. Between 1950 and 1973 economic growth in western Europe, at 4.6 per cent per annum, was more than twice that from 1913 to 1950 or from 1973 to 1993, and GDP per capita grew more rapidly than in any other comparably large group of countries in the world. These three decades comprised *les trente glorieuses*—'the glorious thirty' (a term coined by the

French demographer Jean Fourastié in 1979)—that transformed not just postwar France but postwar Europe as a whole.

Europe's postwar transformation comprised four key elements:

The first was making good the damage left by the war. This dominated the phase of reconstruction during the second half of the 1940s, and by 1951 GDP across western Europe had recovered to its highest prewar levels. Recovery from war damage allowed European economies to reclaim their 'natural level' after the effects of interwar depression and wartime destruction.

The second was the augmentation of the labour supply. Despite the war losses, European societies found new reserves of labour: from among the unemployed; from more women working outside the home (especially in eastern Europe); from the movement of people from agriculture and the countryside into the towns; and from the migration of workers from East to West Germany, from southern to northern Europe, and to Europe from colonies or former colonies.

The third was state involvement in economic management and investment. This occurred to a greater or lesser extent across western Europe, as the state was mobilized to promote modernization, to channel the development of private enterprises, and in some cases to take whole sectors into public ownership. In eastern Europe comprehensive, direct state control and comprehensive planning was imposed.

The fourth was military spending. Despite the end of a war economy in 1945, the confrontation across the 'Iron Curtain' and the wars fought by western European powers against anti-colonial movements fuelled substantial military expenditure. In the economic as well as the political sphere, postwar Europe did not really leave war behind.

Although factories across Europe had been damaged by bombing and fighting on the ground, much productive capacity had actually remained intact. The postwar slump in industrial production was caused not so much by wholesale wartime destruction as by disruption to transport, supply chains, and distribution. Thus the immediate task was to bring surviving industrial capacity back into production, which meant that key challenges revolved around transport and coal supply. In May 1945 Europe's port facilities, railways, bridges, roads, and waterways were barely functioning. The majority of Europe's rail freight wagons had been damaged or destroyed; water transport was crippled with waterways blocked and a lack of barges; railways, roads, and bridges were unusable. In the British Occupation Zone of Germany, which contained the country's largest industrial region and coal reserves, just 1,000 out of 13,000 kilometres of railway track were usable at the war's end (but 12,000 kilometres were back in operation by the middle of 1946).

Getting coal out of the ground was a critical concern. At the end of 1947 West German coal output was still only 52 per cent of 1938 levels; and coal production in Europe as a whole was 20 per cent below prewar. While underground mines in Belgium, France, and Germany survived the war in remarkably good condition, their above-ground installations had suffered substantial damage. (To the east, mines in the Donetsk region of Ukraine had been damaged due to deliberate German destruction.) The availability of labour was also a major problem, not least since much of the housing in mining regions had been bombed. In France and Belgium German prisoners of war were deployed: in Belgium more than 50,000 German prisoners were working in the mines at the end of 1945; and in France a third of the roughly 900,000 Germans in French captivity to 1948 were deployed in mines.

Wartime damage was not limited to industry or to urban areas. In many rural regions roads, rail lines, and large swathes of agricultural land had been damaged by military action, and fertilizer and farm machinery were in short supply. In 1946 European agricultural production was less than two-thirds what it had been in 1938; in 1947 agricultural output was even a bit lower—a result of the extremely cold winter of 1946/7, followed by drought in the spring and summer. In addition, farmers were often reluctant to deliver food to the cities (in exchange for currency at a time of high inflation). The consequences were catastrophic. According to United Nations experts, in 1946 more than 140 million Europeans had to survive on less than 2,000 calories per day, and another 100 million on less than 1,500; in Germany, daily rations officially stood at 1,550 calories, but as late as 1948 Germans' actual rations in fact were only about 1,000 calories per day—not even one-third of what was reckoned to be the requirement of a physically active man. In Ukraine in 1946–7 famine claimed the lives of a million people.

Given the problems of food supply, it may seem surprising that a significant feature of Europe's postwar economic development was the movement of millions of people from farm to town. Yet as agriculture became more mechanized and productive, former rural dwellers supplied labour needed for rapidly growing industrial and service sectors. Between 1955 and 1975 migration from agriculture would become the largest source of dependent non-agricultural employment growth in the EEC. In Italy this helped to fuel the phenomenal growth of the industrial economy during the 1950s and 1960s: in 1950 two-fifths of those working in Italy were employed in agriculture, but by 1977 the comparable figure was just 16 per cent. In France almost three in 10 employed people worked on the farm in 1950, but in 1971 the share of the economically active population employed in agriculture was less than 10 per cent. In eastern Europe (where already between 1948 and 1953 the industrial workforce expanded by roughly one-third, with much of this expansion coming from people who previously had worked on the land) the decline was no less steep: in Poland, just after the war roughly half of the male workforce still worked in agriculture, but by 1980 the proportion was a little over a quarter; in Romania the comparable reduction was from 61.7 per cent in

1950 to 19.5 per cent in 1980; and in Bulgaria there was a decline from 63.2 to 17.2 per cent over the same period.

A further source of labour in (western) Europe was immigrants. In Britain 1,773,000 immigrant workers arrived between 1945 and 1970, mostly from India, Pakistan, and Ireland. In France, nearly a million Europeans (the *pieds-noirs*) arrived from Algeria as it approached independence in 1962, and in 1973–4 there were roughly 450,000 Algerians, 230,000 Italians, 120,000 Moroccans, 380,000 Portuguese, and 270,000 Spaniards living in the country. West Germany benefited from the arrival of well over three million compatriots from the GDR until the Berlin Wall was erected in August 1961. In Switzerland the number of foreign workers increased from 50,000 in 1946 to 721,000 in 1964, and at the beginning of the 1970s they comprised about a quarter of the entire labour force.

War breeds inflation. Much of the costs of the Second World War had been met by borrowing and printing money, and postwar governments then attempted to rebuild their economies and to meet acute social needs through deficit spending, which fuelled continued inflation. (In 1946 budget deficits in the UK, France, and Italy comprised nearly a tenth of national income, and in Belgium and the Netherlands they were even higher.) Attempts were made to control prices through continued rationing. By the end of 1948, butter, meat, and sugar were rationed in 15 European countries; bread and petrol were rationed in 14; coffee in 12; and coal and textiles in 11. This, however, fuelled black markets, where prices soared.

Inflation plagued virtually the whole of Europe in the early postwar years. In France, which faced widespread shortages, low production levels, and a thriving black market after liberation, and where the government turned to substantial deficit spending, postwar inflation rose to over 50 per cent. In 1945 wholesale prices in France were more than four and a half times their 1938 levels;

by 1946 they were eight times as high; by 1948 nearly 20 times; and by 1950 24 times. The French franc's value on foreign exchanges fell accordingly.

Italy's economy too was in poor shape when the war ended. However, by 1948 Italian manufacturing had reached prewar levels, and by 1950 the same was true of Italian agriculture. To help pay for this recovery the state provided cheap credit, boosting the money supply. Consequently the wholesale price index (already at a level 26 times what it had been in 1938) more than doubled between June 1946 and September 1947 (after which economic policy was reversed). In the Netherlands, German wartime occupation policies that had quadrupled the money supply led to rampant inflation, leaving postwar Dutch governments with a difficult task of stabilizing prices.

By contrast, postwar inflation in the UK was relatively modest—rising from 2.8 per cent in 1945 and 3.1 per cent in 1946 to 7 per cent in 1947 and 7.7 per cent in 1948, but falling back to 2.8 per cent in 1949 (before rising again in 1950 and 1951, during the Korean War). Nevertheless, prices there had risen by 50 per cent during the six years of war and a further 35 per cent in the first six years of peace, meaning that UK prices doubled between 1939 and 1951. And in Belgium, which emerged from the war in relatively good economic shape, monetary reform and control of the money supply helped to control postwar inflation.

In eastern Europe the challenge posed by inflation was also substantial. The most extreme episode occurred in Hungary, which between August 1945 and July 1946 experienced the worst inflation ever recorded: during the last week of July 1946 prices were rising by over 150,000 per cent *daily*; and when currency stabilization was achieved with the monetary reform of 1 August 1946, the new currency was exchanged for the old at a rate of 400 *octillion* to one. However, across the eastern bloc a regime of non-convertible currencies and fixed prices of basic goods, supported by state subsidies, was instituted. Judged by official indices, after the early 1950s price stability was remarkable: between 1955 and 1975 the consumer price index actually fell in the GDR; in several other countries it rose by less than 0.5 per cent annually, with the highest average annual increase of roughly 1.5 per cent recorded in Poland. Yet all was not quite what it seemed. Official indices omitted prices on free markets; in economies characterized by the scarcity of many consumer goods, free or black-market prices and bribery increased the actual (unrecorded) cost of living; and from the 1970s rising inflation helped to undermine the popular legitimacy of eastern Europe's socialist regimes, most notably in Poland.

A major problem facing European economies during the early postwar years was a shortage of dollars. The United States emerged from the war as the world's main creditor and the linchpin of the system of fixed exchange rates established following the Bretton Woods Agreement of 1944. War-damaged European countries needed dollars to pay for imported goods, yet found it difficult to export to earn these dollars. A response to the problem was devaluation. In September 1949 the UK devalued Sterling by nearly one-third (from $4.03 to $2.80 to the pound), and others followed suit: the Scandinavian countries, the Netherlands, and Greece devalued by a similar amount; Belgium, France, West Germany, and Portugal by somewhat less; and the Italian lira was allowed to fluctuate and thus to depreciate against the dollar. This improved European countries' terms of trade vis-à-vis the USA, and the devaluations of 1949 improved their export prospects and thus the prospects for economic growth.

The early postwar years also saw some European states nationalize sectors of the economy. In France, the Constituent Assembly (elected in October 1945) passed acts to nationalize the banks in December 1945, electric power and gas in March 1946, and insurance as well as coal in April 1946; the nationalization of the French mines had begun already in December 1944. In the UK, the

Labour government embarked on a comprehensive programme of nationalization: of the Bank of England in 1946, the coal industry at the beginning of 1947, the railways at the beginning of 1948, the electricity industry a few months later; in 1946 the National Health Service Act was passed into law (with the NHS coming into being in July 1948), waterways and electricity came into public ownership in 1947, gas in 1948, and iron and steel in 1949. By 1951 more than two million workers in the UK were employed in public corporations. However, commitment to direct public ownership was not universal. After the massive intervention in the economy by the Nazi and fascist states, in Germany and Italy there was less enthusiasm to extend state direct control.

No discussion of postwar economic recovery in Europe can overlook the Marshall Plan (to give it its proper name, the European Recovery Program), which led to the USA transferring $13 billion to Europe's war-damaged economies between 1948 and 1951. This helped European countries to overcome their shortage of dollars and thus to finance necessary imports, stimulate productive investment, and repair damaged infrastructure. There has been disagreement over the extent to which European economic recovery depended on Marshall Plan aid—with the traditional view that it allowed reconstruction to take place and thus precipitated postwar Europe's Golden Age first being challenged by Alan Milward in the mid-1980s. Nevertheless, while the quantitative impact of Marshall Plan aid itself may have been relatively modest, others have pointed to its more indirect effects. These included strengthening commitments to the market economy and trade liberalization, contributing to political and financial stability and creating an attractive environment for investment, thus bringing existing capacity back into production and allowing Europe to overcome the war's negative effects on economic growth more rapidly than otherwise possible.

Countries that received large amounts of Marshall aid recovered more quickly than those that had not, and between 1947 and 1951 industrial output in the countries that participated in the Marshall Plan rose by 55 per cent. The Marshall Plan also committed the participating countries to a market economy and parliamentary democracy and provided a basis for the liberal economic consensus between capital, labour, and the state in postwar western Europe.

However much the Marshall Plan itself was responsible for economic recovery in western Europe, there can be little doubt that postwar recovery was swift—to the surprise of many contemporary observers. Nevertheless, it was only towards the second half of the 1950s that one could begin to speak of a 'consumer society' having arrived. Even in the great success story of West Germany, while conditions improved after the hardships of the first postwar years, it was not really until the late 1950s and early 1960s that employee households were able to escape the frugality with which they had had to manage their budgets and to emerge into the world of consumer choice.

In the countries of the Iberian peninsula and in the socialist half of the continent (where regimes did not accept the conditions that would have allowed them to participate in the Marshall Plan) living standards remained lower for longer. In Spain, where the effects of the Civil War, initial reluctance of western countries to cooperate with the Franco regime, and continued attempts to promote autarky crippled the economy, living standards remained below those in its western European neighbours. While its economy recovered somewhat during the 1950s, only after economic reforms had been instituted towards the end of that decade did Spain enter an unparalleled phase of industrialization and prosperity.

After the immediate postwar years, Europe's economies grew at unprecedented rates. During the 1950s the annual average compound growth rate for western Europe was 4.4 per cent, and during the 1960s it was 5.2 per cent. GDP per capita grew steadily. During the 1950s unemployment as a percentage of the labour force rapidly declined, and during the 1960s it averaged only 1.5 per cent across much of western Europe. In West Germany, it stood at a mere 0.8 per cent over the 1960s. Steady work became a new feature in the lives of millions of Europeans, and workers recruited from less prosperous regions in southern Europe benefited from the increasing material prosperity of the host countries. For Europeans scarred by memories of depression and mass unemployment in the 1930s, the achievement of what was, in effect, full employment could seem miraculous.

The postwar economic transformation was particularly remarkable in Italy and (West) Germany. In Italy, more than two million people had been recorded officially as unemployed in 1950. Then between 1950 and 1963 Italian industrial production rose by an average of 8.1 per cent annually, and by 1966 it was three times what it had been in 1951. Fiat became one of Europe's largest manufacturers of motor vehicles, producing nearly nine million cars between 1961 and 1970 and selling more cars in 1967 even than Volkswagen; and Olivetti produced nearly a million typewriters per year. Italian GDP per capita rose and living standards visibly improved. Italy achieved its postwar *miracolo economico*.

Like Italy, Germany experienced considerable inflation just after the war. Policies instituted to control inflation (with the introduction of the Deutschmark in June 1948) led initially to a rapid rise in unemployment, which rose to two million (13.3 per cent of the workforce) by January 1950. The FRG then benefited from the boom caused by the Korean War. Between 1950 and 1961 West German economic growth averaged 8.3 per cent; exports rose and unemployment fell; between 1950 and 1963 the nominal net income of an employee more than doubled, and between 1950 and 1973 it more than trebled in real terms. By the end of the 1950s the FRG had become the world's third largest steel producer and third largest shipbuilder. Understandably, Germans regarded what they experienced as a *Wirtschaftswunder*.

Hardly less miraculous was the growth in other countries damaged by war. GDP per capita in Austria, which had been part of the 'Greater German Reich' between 1938 and 1945, increased by a factor of three between 1950 and 1973. Spain, whose economy had been stagnant and much of whose population endured acute poverty during the 1940s, experienced its own 'economic miracle' as economic growth galloped ahead between 1961 and 1973 at an annual rate of 7.3 per cent in real terms; by 1973 Spain's GDP per capita had increased more than three and a half times since 1950. From a rather higher base, real GDP in France increased three and a half times between 1952 and 1979.

Western Europe's 'miracle years' were characterized not simply by a revival of heavy industry (e.g. coal, iron and steel, shipbuilding), but by a huge expansion of the service sector. Postwar western European economies became increasingly service based, and employment in the tertiary sector grew substantially in both relative and absolute terms. By the end of the 1970s a majority of employees in the UK, France, West Germany, the Benelux countries, Switzerland, Austria, and Scandinavia were working in services including transport, financial services, communications, and public administration. The growth in public-sector employment was fuelled by an expanding welfare state, which provided relatively well-paid, secure jobs as well as increasing benefits to increasing numbers of Europeans.

Higher living standards were reflected in the growth of international tourism. Before the postwar boom, if Europeans had experienced foreign countries it was often either in uniform, as forced labourers, or as refugees. However, from the late 1950s, as disposable income grew and holiday time increased for millions of Europeans, mass tourism became both a driver of economic growth and visible evidence of the transition from scarcity to plenty. International tourism proved particularly important for southern Europe, which could offer sun and sand to better-off inhabitants in countries to the north. Italy became the continent's

8. August 1966 at the Spanish holiday resort of Benidorm, packed with 20,000 visitors, mostly foreigners. Ten years previously it had been a tiny fishing village.

largest recipient of international tourists by the late 1960s, and Spain saw an eightfold increase in the number of tourists visiting the country between 1959 and 1973. Rising disposable incomes could be spent on Spanish beaches, in Italian trattorias, French bistros, and Swiss and Austrian ski resorts (Figure 8).

The economic trajectory of eastern Europe diverged from those to the west in a number of respects. While unemployment in western Europe generally was much lower than in the prewar years, in the planned economies of eastern Europe there was almost no officially recognized unemployment at all. This reflected a greater reliance on labour inputs, involving the employment of considerably higher proportions of the female population and of people over 65: in 1970 participation rates among women and workers over 65 were estimated by the International Labour Organization to be 69.8 per cent and 15.1 per cent respectively in the GDR but only 48.2 per cent and 9.7 per cent respectively in the FRG; in Poland in 1970 71.2 per cent of women and 41.8 per cent of the population over 65 were estimated to be in employment. (Only at the end of the 1970s did female participation rates in Sweden and Denmark match eastern European levels, reaching just over 70 per cent.)

While the socialist states of eastern Europe mobilized high proportions of their adult population into the labour force, they emphasized industrial production at the expense of services. As the output of coal and iron ore declined in the old industrial centres of western Europe—in the UK, Belgium, West Germany, and France—it increased in Poland, Czechoslovakia, and the GDR (with deleterious consequences for the environment). Centralized economic planning delivered rapid growth in heavy industry, but it also led to inefficient production, serious shortages of consumer goods, and economic stagnation (notably in Czechoslovakia in the early 1960s) which attempts at reform failed to rectify. Despite discussion during the 1960s of a possible 'convergence' of eastern and western European economic systems and eastern European debates about managerial reform (associated with Ota Šik in Czechoslovakia and Evsei Liberman in the USSR), divergence remained.

Nevertheless, at least until problems inherent in centralized socialist planning and the effects of the oil price rises of 1973 and the early 1980s made themselves felt, living standards generally rose in eastern Europe. National income, income per capita, consumer expenditure, consumption, and indices of social welfare pointed to a rise in people's welfare in the 'People's Democracies'. Yet difficulties remained: there were chronic shortages of quality goods that consumers desired, and living standards of eastern Europeans lagged behind those of their western counterparts—which remained a point of comparison and a source of popular discontent.

An important part of the economic success of western Europe was the huge increase in trade following the Second World War.

The experience of the interwar period, when trade barriers had been erected as European states sought protection within currency blocs and were attracted to autarky, provided a negative precedent. Instead postwar states looked to multilateral trade and currency convertibility to provide bases for reconstruction and growth. Marshall Plan aid facilitated these goals, as did subsequent steps towards European economic integration. After the creation of the ECSC in 1951 and the EEC in 1957 (and, to a lesser extent, the European Free Trade Association in 1960), barriers to trade among European states were progressively dismantled. Between 1950 and 1973, western European trade grew by more than 8 per cent annually, as trade liberalization allowed individual countries to exploit comparative advantage, gain access to larger markets, and become more attractive for investment. The dismantling of tariff barriers and opening up of larger markets for western European producers promoted economic integration and with it further economic growth—developments that continued with the expansion of the EEC in the 1970s (with the accession of the UK, Ireland, and Denmark in 1973) and the 1980s (Greece in 1981 and Portugal and Spain in 1986), through the realization of the EU's Single European Market in 1993 and the adoption of the euro as the currency in much of the EU at the end of the 20th century.

In socialist eastern Europe until the mid-1950s foreign trade was regarded as something of a necessary evil, and generally organized on a bilateral basis. Nevertheless, after the eastern European states had declined to participate in the Marshall Plan programme, some effort to promote regional economic integration and augment trade followed. In 1949 the USSR created the Council for Mutual Economic Assistance (CMEA, more commonly referred to as Comecon, which lasted until 1991), which in effect promoted regional economic autarky within the eastern bloc. Trade grew, but most of it—between 60 and 75 per cent—occurred within the bloc. During the 1960s, with the introduction of economic reforms, greater interest was shown in foreign trade, which increased during the 1970s: whereas the eastern European socialist countries

(Albania, Bulgaria, Czechoslovakia, the GDR, Hungary, Poland, Romania, and the USSR) accounted for a mere 5 per cent of world trade in 1948, during the 1970s the figure fluctuated between 8 and 9 per cent.

In western Europe during the 1950s and 1960s there seemed ample justification for British Prime Minister Harold Macmillan's famous assertion, made at a Conservative Party rally in July 1957, that 'most of our people have never had it so good'. Real incomes rose rapidly, as wages and earnings rose significantly faster than prices. Homes of workers became stocked with durable goods that had been beyond the reach of their parents a couple of decades earlier. In the FRG, only 7 per cent of households possessed an electric cooker in 1950, but eight years later the comparable figure was 32 per cent; in 1955 one in 10 of West German households possessed a fridge, in 1962/3 more than half did. In the UK, by 1961 three-quarters of families had a television set, and by 1971 the figure had risen to 91 per cent; while only 1.5 million UK households had a private telephone in 1951, the comparable figure in 1966 was 4.2 million; and in 1971 64 per cent of UK families had a washing machine. Many Europeans no doubt shared the feelings of a woman, born in 1924 and raised in a working-class district of Hamburg, who (in an interview in 1990) enthused over her 'new modern kitchen'—complete with an electric cooker and a fridge purchased with credit—when she moved into a new dwelling in 1957: 'it was simply fantastic'.

Millions of Europeans could also afford a motor vehicle for the first time. Between 1950 and 1973 the annual sales of cars in Europe increased from 1,595,000 to 13,280,000. In the UK, which had something of a head start, motor-vehicle ownership grew from 2,307,000 cars and vans in 1950 to 3,609,000 in 1955, 5,650,000 in 1960, 9,131,000 in 1965, and 11,802,000 in 1970. By 1965 car ownership in France had reached nearly 10 million, in West Germany 9 million, and in Italy more than 5 million.

The expansion of the motor-vehicle industry was a major element of western Europe's postwar economic growth, with the phenomenal success of Volkswagen (whose factory at its headquarters in Wolfsburg grew to become the largest in the world), BMW, Ford, Opel (a GM company), and Daimler-Benz in West Germany; Renault, Citroën, and Peugeot in France; Fiat in Italy; Volvo in Sweden. At the same time, mass motorization had its down side: in France, for example, between 1945 and 1973 250,000 people were killed in motor-vehicle accidents (memorably portrayed by Jean-Luc Godard in his 1967 film *Weekend*, with its traffic jams and violent car crashes).

With the arrival of the postwar affluent society, western Europeans increasingly saw themselves as consumers. As incomes grew, the proportion required for basic needs diminished. At the same time, the working day grew shorter, the five-day working week became the rule, and employees had more holidays. The arrival of a 'consumer society' meant that Europeans no longer just purchased what they *needed*; increasingly they could choose what they *wanted*. This coincided with a growing focus on brands—an expression of choice in consumer goods and of individual taste. As supermarkets and self-service stores began to spread across the continent, decreasing proportions of increasing incomes were spent on necessities and larger proportions on discretionary purchases. In the FRG, for example, the proportion of household expenditure spent on food declined from 43.0 per cent in 1950 to 30.6 per cent 20 years later. (During the same period the portion spent on rent increased from 7.2 per cent to 12.5 per cent, and to 16.4 per cent in 1980.) For those who had lived through the interwar economic crises, war, and postwar austerity, the *trente glorieuses* signalled the arrival of a world of plenty, something that their children increasingly took for granted.

In eastern Europe living standards also improved, but less than in the west. Incomes rose across socialist eastern Europe during the 1950s and 1960s—albeit generally from a lower base than in the west. Disposable money incomes per capita increased by 130.2 per cent between 1955 and 1973 in the GDR and by 145.7 per cent in Czechoslovakia (the two most developed of the socialist states), and by 348.8 per cent in Bulgaria and by 371.1 per cent in Poland. This was paralleled by growing expenditure on consumer durables, and by the mid-1970s the inhabitants of eastern Europe too had begun to purchase washing machines, cookers, and black-and-white televisions in large numbers.

However, the degree to which higher money incomes led to higher living standards in eastern Europe is difficult to measure. While the prices of most goods required day to day were kept artificially low, citizens of socialist countries had to contend with rising prices on unofficial, free markets, of second-hand goods, and of goods available largely or solely on the black market. Goods in high demand were often in short supply, as socialist enterprises were less responsive to consumer demand and shortages of foreign currency limited imports. Attempts to offer socialist citizens a taste of the west with selected imports could not mask the inadequacies of the socialist consumer model; and while allowing socialist citizens to make purchases in foreign-currency shops served to soak up foreign currency circulating privately, it also highlighted the second-class nature of the non-convertible currency with which they were paid.

Among eastern Europe's socialist states Yugoslavia was an exception, charting its own path following the break with Stalin after the Second World War. It abandoned its centralized economic planning system in favour of decentralized decision-making, and its economy grew rapidly. However, this led to inflation, which set in substantially from the early 1960s: consumer price inflation increased from 4.3 per cent in 1956–60 and 7.8 per cent in 1960–3 to 13.0 per cent in 1963–70 and 17.5 per cent in 1975. Unlike the states of the Soviet bloc, Yugoslavia saw significant unemployment (rising to slightly over 10 per cent of the resident labour force in 1975), and was linked more directly to capitalist Europe as large numbers of Yugoslavs (some 800,000, or 15 per cent, of the labour force) found employment outside the country.

Europe's Golden Age came to an end in the 1970s, as the extraordinary factors that had underpinned the postwar economic miracles evaporated. The system of fixed exchange rates that had provided currency stability for decades effectively ended when its linchpin, the dollar, left the gold standard in August 1971. The era of low-priced oil, from which postwar economies had profited as they became increasingly reliant on oil for their energy needs, came to an abrupt end with the quadrupling of the oil price by OPEC (Organization of the Petroleum Exporting Countries) between October 1973 and March 1974. The reconstruction that had driven postwar economic growth had largely been completed; wage pressures grew, leading to rising inflation; unemployment rose to levels not seen for decades in western Europe and even more so in southern Europe, undermining living standards and weakening trade unions; the 'golden age of welfare states' was undermined by changing demographic structures and slowing economic growth; and to the east the rigidities and wastefulness of centralized planning caught up with a socialist economic model ill equipped to deal with the steep rise in oil prices. After a postwar boom that many had believed could continue forever, Europe entered an era of 'stagflation'—of stagnant growth and high unemployment combined with inflation.

The end of the Golden Age was followed by the reversal of assumptions that had governed Europe's economic development during the previous quarter-century. Keynesian policies of demand management were called into question in the face of 'stagflation', and in eastern Europe the socialist system of state control and economic planning stuttered and then collapsed. With public debt mounting, with shrinking proportions of the population of working age having to support growing proportions in retirement, with increased overseas competition (especially from Asia), and new technological developments undermining the old industrial economies, the postwar economic models seemed to have reached the end of the road.

Keynesian policies were jettisoned in favour of supply-side economics. First to travel down this path was the UK. Although the Labour government of James Callaghan and Denis Healey (1976–9) began the retreat from assumptions that had governed economic policy over the previous 30 years, it was the government of Margaret Thatcher from 1979 that turned away decisively from the postwar consensus. The direct role of the state in the economy was to be pared back, with deregulation and a comprehensive programme of privatization (although it should be remembered that the Labour government had already sold the state's share of British Petroleum in 1976). Among the publicly owned assets sold off were telecommunications, energy utilities, air transport, and much of the country's council-housing stock. At the same time, the numbers of British unemployed increased to levels far higher than those seen for decades.

Other European countries moved in a similar direction. In France, the socialist François Mitterrand, elected President in 1981, initially pursued a programme of nationalization and increased social benefits (e.g. pensions, family, maternity, and housing allowances, as well as increases in the minimum wage). However, in 1983, after unemployment and inflation continued to rise and the franc was devalued repeatedly, Mitterrand (with his Economics and Finance Minister Jacques Delors) opted for a *tournant de la rigueur* (austerity turn): tax rises and public spending cuts, privatization (e.g. of the major banks and the large oil companies Total and Elf), and economic liberalization. Consequently, inflation plummeted, from an annual average of 9.6 per cent during 1981–5 to 3.1 per cent during 1986–90, while unemployment remained stubbornly high. (The figures for the EC as a whole were 9.1 per cent in 1981–5 and 4.3 per cent in 1986–90 for inflation, and 9.8 per cent in 1981–5 and 10.0 per cent in 1986–90 for unemployment.)

Post-Franco Spain followed a different route to a similar destination. The Spanish government elected in 1982 and headed by the socialist Felipe González eschewed socialist intervention. Having observed developments in France, González decided not to follow the path initially chosen by Mitterrand and instead sought to control inflation and make the country more attractive to foreign investment. The results were similar to what occurred in France from 1983: falling inflation (11.7 per cent annually in 1982–5 to 6.5 per cent in 1986–90) combined with high unemployment (19.1 per cent in 1982–5 rising to 20.9 per cent in 1986–90). Seeking membership in the EC, the Spanish government saw its main economic task as achieving 'convergence' with countries in the EC, in terms of inflation, government spending, and debt.

In West Germany, which had weathered the storms of the 1970s better than most, the challenges posed by inflation and rising unemployment—Federal government expenditure on unemployment benefit nearly trebled between 1977 and 1982—also led to rethinking. This was reflected in the political *Wende* ('turn') of 1982 (whereby the Social–Liberal coalition headed by the Social Democrat Helmut Schmidt was replaced by a coalition headed by the Christian Democrat Helmut Kohl), and articulated by the liberal (Free Democrat) Federal Economics Minister Otto Graf Lambsdorff in his proposals for dealing with 'the current employment and growth crisis', the aim of which was to combat the growth of public spending and to cut taxes.

In Sweden, the economic-welfare model that Social Democratic governments had built over decades and that had created what one observer termed 'the best society that has ever existed in the world', held out a bit longer. However, maintaining the Swedish model proved increasingly difficult. The money required for pensions and subsidies mushroomed, the proportion of the labour force working in the public sector rose steeply, and taxation increased so that by 1990 more than half the average Swedish family's income went to the state. Economic growth slowed and inflation rose—to 10 per cent in 1990. In response, Social Democratic Prime Minister Ingvar Carlsson (who became Prime Minister following the assassination of Olaf Palme in 1986) opted for privatizing public services, cutting back the welfare state, and implementing a tax reform that reduced the marginal tax rate. His successor, the Moderate Carl Bildt, took the 'counter-revolution' further, cutting taxes and reducing social benefits. Yet the economy continued to shrink; unemployment rose steeply (to 12.5 per cent in 1993); and in November 1992 the government floated the krona (which immediately lost 20 per cent of its value). It was not until 1994 that growth returned.

For eastern Europe, the challenges led not just to painful readjustment, but to the crumbling of the economic system. During the 1970s and 1980s the economies of the Soviet bloc were subject to many of the same pressures as were their western neighbours: inflation, rising energy prices, the increasing cost of social-welfare programmes, growing numbers of the elderly, the need to shift from investment in heavy industry to new technologies, and external (hard-currency) debt. However, the Soviet bloc countries had to address these challenges within a more rigid political and economic system. Attempts during the 1960s to introduce market mechanisms into socialist planned economies had been limited and/or stillborn; attempts during the 1970s to focus more on 'the growing material and cultural needs of working people' fell short of the mark. While the old industries in the west were being dismantled and just-in-time production introduced, eastern Europe remained largely wedded to the industrial model imposed during the early postwar years. Seeking a passage from scarcity to plenty, 'real-existing socialism' stumbled. Its shortcomings were painfully apparent during the 1970s and 1980s: polluted industrial landscapes, shoddy consumer goods, and drab and poorly constructed housing. In sum, the postwar socialist planned economy proved unable to provide a successful alternative to the west's consumerist model.

9. Fiat car dealer in Wrocław, Poland, in September 1978.

Eastern European countries looked west to solve the problem: the largest single investment in the USSR's 1966–70 five-year plan was a giant car factory in Togliattigrad, where a version of the Fiat 124 was assembled (to be sold in the west as Lada and in the Soviet Union as Zhiguli); and in Poland the 'Polski Fiat' was produced under licence from the Italian manufacturer between 1968 and 1991 (Figure 9). During the 1970s and 1980s eastern European states attempted to compensate for shortcomings in indigenous technological investment and the provision of consumer goods by borrowing hard currency. Their debt quadrupled between 1975 and 1989, from 18.8 to 79.9 billion dollars, the lion's share between 1975 and 1980. Hungary and Poland took on most of this debt. However, this did not rescue the system, and in the Soviet bloc only Romania's leadership was willing to squeeze domestic living standards in order to liquidate foreign debt—which contributed to the unpopularity of Nicolae Ceaușescu's regime and to his bloody end in 1989.

The collapse of the state-socialist economic system was greeted at the time with no small degree of triumphalism in the west.

However, viewed over three decades later, it appears that both east and west were shaken by some similar challenges as the period of postwar recovery and reconstruction came to an end and as economic growth stalled in the 1970s and 1980s. Nevertheless, much had changed for the better. Living standards across Europe were far higher in the 1970s and 1980s than they had been in the 1950s. Europeans enjoyed greatly improved social-welfare programmes and pensions; they were better housed; they were better educated; they had more leisure; they were better nourished; they lived longer. For tens of millions of Europeans, austerity had been left behind and plenty had become the new normal.

Europe's remarkable postwar journey from scarcity to plenty framed the ways in which Europeans remembered the postwar era. The experience of hardship and austerity after the war, the rebuilding of a shattered continent, the metaphors of 'economic miracle' and 'the 30 glorious years', the spread of the welfare state and consumer society, the end of the unprecedented economic boom of the 1950s and 1960s, the reverberations of the oil-price shock of 1973, the crumbling of the postwar Keynesian consensus of successful demand management in the 1970s and 1980s, the collapse of the socialist economic model, and the triumph of the west over the east—these broadly framed Europeans' understanding of the postwar epoch. While cyclical fluctuations had continued to occur, these were comparatively mild, and between 1950 and 1970 GDP did not decline in any European country. Looking back upon the postwar era, Europeans generally could see that they had become more prosperous and secure.

Yet individual experiences of the postwar decades were hardly uniform. Not only did they differ between east and west, north and south; they also differed between men and women, young and old, rich and poor. No less importantly, the experience of Europe's postwar era differed by generational cohort:

Those born in the late 19th and early 20th century had experienced two world wars and postwar crises as adults. For them, war-related declines in living standards, malnourishment, and inflation were not new; their expectations were framed by what had happened after the First World War, when much of Europe was plagued by economic crisis and inflation, and then by the great depression that had scarred their middle years.

For those born in the first two decades of the 20th century, childhood and coming of age had been marked by war and economic crisis, adulthood by dictatorship for some and apparent economic improvement, until that was destroyed through the Second World War.

For those born during the 1920s and early 1930s, the shock of the war and the extreme hardships of the first postwar years came as they emerged into adulthood, to be followed by the economic upswing of the 1950s and 1960s as they were in their most productive years. This was the generation for whom the postwar economic 'miracle' made a most powerful impression, after experiencing the economic catastrophes of the interwar period, the war and the immediate postwar years, and then benefiting powerfully from the postwar economic boom. Members of this generation also bid their farewell to public, productive lives as the postwar era came to a close, in many cases leaving the labour force due either to losing their jobs and/or taking early retirement during the 1980s.

For those born in the late 1930s and during the war, having experienced the economic catastrophes of the war years and the hardships of the early postwar years as children, the transformation from scarcity to plenty defined their coming of age and adult lives.

However, it was the postwar generation—the 'baby boomers'— who were the great beneficiaries of the economic boom that followed the Second World War. For this generation, childhood, adolescence, and young adulthood unfolded in a world of increasing economic opportunity and prosperity. Fear of unemployment and severe material hardship was notably absent. They had inherited a plentiful new world, built in large measure through the hard work of their elders. Theirs was a privileged generation that more than any other profited from the boom of the 1950s and 1960s and that continued to profit from it into retirement. Whereas the older generations that had experienced economic crisis and severe hardship desperately wanted to achieve economic security after the war, for the postwar generation prosperity became almost self-evident, even as growth spluttered in the 1970s. As memories of scarcity faded, plenty became the normality of postwar Europe.

Chapter 7
The Cold War, nationalism, and the transformation of European politics

European states emerged after the Second World War diminished in power within the 'straitjacket of the Cold War', and the confrontation between two antagonistic blocs down the middle of the continent dominated their foreign policy and politics.

At the centre of this confrontation were the Cold War military alliances, the origins of which date from the immediate postwar years. They had arisen against a background of concern about a possible German resurgence and rising tensions between east and west. In the west this development began with the renewal of the Anglo-French alliance in the Treaty of Dunkirk in March 1947, with American President Truman's declaration (the 'Truman Doctrine', also in March 1947) 'that it must be the policy of the United States to support free peoples who are resisting subjugation by armed minorities or by outside pressures' (responding in the first instance to communist pressure in Greece and Turkey), and with the UK and France joining the Benelux countries in the Treaty of Brussels in March 1948 (calling for 'economic, social and cultural collaboration and collective self-defence'). In the east the formal process was signalled with the conclusion in 1949 of mutual assistance treaties between the USSR on the one hand and Bulgaria, Czechoslovakia, Hungary, Poland, and Romania on the other (granting the USSR the right to extend its military presence on the territory of its eastern European allies).

These initiatives were followed by the establishment of formal military alliances which were dominated by the two superpowers and cemented the presence of the USA in Europe's postwar military architecture. The treaty creating NATO was signed on 4 April 1949 by the USA, the UK, France, and the Benelux countries, as well as Canada, Portugal, Italy, Norway, Denmark, and Iceland; the treaty creating the Warsaw Pact (the Warsaw Treaty Organization, WTO, officially the Treaty of Friendship, Cooperation, and Mutual Assistance) was signed by the USSR and seven other eastern European socialist republics on 14 May 1955, a few days after West Germany had become a NATO member. Membership of these alliances significantly diminished national sovereignty—notably with Article 5 of the NATO Treaty, which stated that an armed attack on one member would be regarded as an attack on all (but leaving it to individual members to take 'such action as necessary, including the use of armed force').

During the early 1950s a more radical plan was put forward for western Europe. In October 1950 France proposed western European military integration, as a way of bringing a future West German army into a European defence architecture under international control, but without the Federal Republic becoming a NATO member. This provided the basis for a treaty to establish a European Defence Community (EDC), which was signed in May 1952 (by France, West Germany, Italy, and the Benelux countries), but never ratified. The EDC project foundered on concerns about national sovereignty: the British were not prepared to join a project which, in the opinion of British Foreign Secretary Anthony Eden, would 'pave the way for a European federation'; neither were the Scandinavian NATO members, and in the wake of defeat in Indochina the French rejected the EDC treaty in August 1954. The idea of a European Defence Community was dead, but its demise paved the way for the FRG to join NATO in May 1955 and develop its own military forces.

In neither east nor west were the structures of the postwar military alliances set in stone. Romania secured the withdrawal of the Soviet Army in 1958 and subsequently pursued policies increasingly independent of Moscow; and France withdrew from NATO's military structure and demanded the removal of US and NATO headquarters and forces from the country in 1966, but remained a member of the alliance. (France rejoined NATO's command structure in 2009.)

Although the UK and France had the strongest military establishments among the postwar western European states and held permanent seats on the UN Security Council, they had difficulty accepting that they now essentially were European rather than world powers. Their limitations were revealed in the Suez Crisis of 1956, when French and British forces responded to Egyptian President Gamal Abdel Nasser's nationalization of the Suez Canal by joining with Israel to attack Egypt and retake the canal. Faced with Soviet threats of retaliation, American pressure to retreat, and losses of currency reserves, the British agreed to a ceasefire without consulting the French. There followed a rapid withdrawal of British and French forces and the resignation of the British Prime Minister Anthony Eden. The days when European states could act as imperial powers and launch such military adventures were over.

Nevertheless the maintenance by Britain and France of substantial military forces and their development of nuclear weapons had attractions for the USA. After the war, the Americans had not wanted to maintain a substantial military footprint in western Europe. According to Eisenhower, the American presence in Europe had been envisaged only as a 'stopgap operation to bring confidence and security to our friends overseas'. A European nuclear deterrent would enable them to defend themselves from a Soviet threat. However, America's assessment soon changed, and in the years to come the USA would station its own missiles armed with nuclear warheads in Europe.

While a sizeable American military presence became a permanent fixture in postwar western Europe, both the UK and France devoted considerable resources to their own nuclear deterrent. The British had collaborated with the USA in developing the atomic bomb during the Second World War, but subsequently were hampered when the Americans restricted their allies' access to further information on nuclear weapons development with the passage of the McMahon Act (Atomic Energy Act) of 1946. Despite economic challenges and the sharp reduction in Britain's armed forces between 1945 and 1950, the Labour government pressed ahead with a British nuclear deterrent. Britain's first nuclear weapons test took place (in Australia) in October 1952, making the UK the world's third nuclear weapons state; the first British thermonuclear (hydrogen) bomb was detonated in May 1957. After the US–UK Mutual Defence Agreement of 1958, however, Britain's nuclear programme developed in collaboration with the USA. With the cancellation in 1960 of Britain's Blue Streak ballistic missile programme and the decision to purchase Polaris submarine missiles from the USA, the UK has not had an independent delivery system for its nuclear weapons, but instead has relied on the USA to maintain its nuclear deterrent.

The French opted for a nuclear weapons programme a few years later and maintained operational independence vis-à-vis the USA. The initial decision to proceed was approved in December 1954 by the administration of the (Centre-Left) Radical Party politician Pierre Mendès-France, but it was Charles de Gaulle who, upon his return to power in 1958, developed the idea of a nuclear *Force de Frappe* that could be deployed independently of NATO. France first tested an atomic bomb (in Algeria) in February 1960; its first nuclear weapons became operational in 1964; and its first thermonuclear bomb was tested (in the South Pacific) in 1968. In contrast to the UK, which came to view its nuclear weapons in conjunction with its American ally, the French government regarded a nuclear deterrent as a means of maintaining an element of military independence.

Through membership in the nuclear club, postwar British and French governments sought to shore up their status as major powers. Yet their stockpiles of nuclear weapons remained relatively small and, consequently, the UK and France in effect remained dependent on their American ally. At the same time, the bomb met with popular opposition in western Europe, where there was anxiety about a renewed outbreak of war. In the UK, the Campaign for Nuclear Disarmament (CND, formed in 1957) held its first public meeting in February 1958 and grew rapidly to over 270 branches in 1959; its Easter marches (the first in 1958 from London to the nuclear weapons facility at Aldermaston, and subsequently in the opposite direction) attracted large numbers of supporters, reaching roughly 150,000 in 1962. In France, many public figures appealed to President de Gaulle in 1959 not to proceed with nuclear weapons tests (to no avail), and by the mid-1960s there was broad opposition on the French left to the country's nuclear deterrent. In the FRG, a number of public figures and theologians (including the country's future President Gustav Heinemann), inspired by the British CND, established the organization *Kampf dem Atomtod* (Fight against Atomic Death) in 1958. They opposed a German acquisition of nuclear weapons, sought the removal of Allied nuclear weapons from German territory, and organized impressive marches in West German cities during the early 1960s; however, none of West Germany's main political parties adopted its position, and by the mid-1960s popular fear of nuclear war had declined.

The military power of the USSR and USA was underpinned by bases on the territory of their European allies. On the eastern side of Europe's Cold War divide, the Soviet Union stationed large numbers of soldiers both to face western armed forces and ensure that its allies not jettison the socialist system and the link with the USSR. (However, the USSR did not maintain its military presence everywhere: it returned to Denmark the island of Bornholm, which Soviet forces had occupied on 9 May 1945 and left on 5 April 1946, and it withdrew its forces from Austria upon the signing of the

State Treaty of 1955.) Large numbers of Soviet troops remained in eastern European countries until the dissolution of the eastern bloc. In the 1980s the USSR maintained roughly 400,000 troops in the GDR, which was the cornerstone of the Soviet Union's strategic military position in central Europe; and when the communist system in Poland collapsed in 1989 approximately 58,000 Soviet troops were still in the country.

On the western side of the divide, while over three million American soldiers had been in Europe in May 1945, most were soon demobilized. However, with rising tensions across the east–west divide, the Berlin Blockade (which began in June 1948, was met with the Berlin Airlift which supplied West Berlin from West Germany, and was lifted in May 1949), and then the outbreak of the Korean War, the American government subsequently committed itself to maintaining significant numbers of troops in western Europe. In the wake of the Korean War, in August 1952 a unified US military command for the European area was established. Between 1950 and the end of 1952 the number of American military personnel stationed in Europe grew to more than 400,000; by June 1954 the US Army in Germany was supplied with atomic artillery; in 1955 the USA established a Southern Europe Task Force in Italy; and a sizeable American military presence remained in Europe through the Cold War years.

Europe itself remained in a state of armed peace throughout the Cold War. While tensions reduced during the 1970s with 'détente', the NATO–Warsaw Pact military confrontation became the largest ever seen in peacetime: in 1987 NATO and the Warsaw Pact in Europe consumed approximately two-thirds of the world's armed forces expenditures, kept millions of men in uniform, and maintained more than 10,000 nuclear warheads. Yet only after the demise of the Warsaw Pact did NATO engage in combat in Europe—first on 28 February 1994, when US warplanes shot down four aircraft of the Serbian Air Force near Banja Luka during the Bosnian War that followed the break-up of Yugoslavia. The change in NATO's role was confirmed in Yugoslavia in the spring of 1999, when its air forces conducted a bombing campaign against Serbia in response to atrocities committed on Albanians in Kosovo; the 78-day campaign involved American and European aircraft—including those of the German Luftwaffe—and was the first large-scale military action in NATO's history.

The integration of Germany into the political and military framework of Europe was central to the continent's postwar history. In the west this meant overcoming a long history of Franco-German conflict. The symbolic moment came in 1962, when Chancellor Konrad Adenauer made an official visit to France in July and joined with President Charles de Gaulle in a mass for peace in the cathedral at Reims—a city heavily damaged by German forces in the First World War and where the Wehrmacht surrendered to the Allies in May 1945. This was followed by de Gaulle's visit to Bonn in September, when the French President was greeted enthusiastically by 200,000 people lining the streets and spoke (in German, which he had learned while a prisoner of war during the First World War) before a crowd on the market square, hailing 'German–French Friendship' (Figure 10). A foundation was laid for a Franco-German relationship at the core of what would become the EU, and was confirmed with the Élysée Treaty of January 1963.

Nevertheless, de Gaulle remained determined to prevent what he regarded as French national interests being subordinated either to the EEC or to the alliance with the USA. And when de Gaulle's successor as President, Georges Pompidou, finally agreed not to block British accession to the Common Market (something that de Gaulle had vetoed in 1963 and again in 1967), this was due in no small measure to French concern that otherwise an increasingly powerful (West) Germany—which was opening up to the east of the continent with its *Ostpolitik*—soon could be in a position to dominate the EEC.

10. President Charles de Gaulle on a two-day visit to Bonn in September 1962.

Among Europe's socialist states, verbal affirmation of internationalism and allegiance to the USSR notwithstanding, national(ist) concerns and sentiment had not evaporated either. Relations between Hungary and Romania were complicated by the presence of a substantial Hungarian minority in the latter, while the Ceauşescu regime in Bucharest sought to create a homogeneous Romanian nation; in Bulgaria, as part of a campaign to create a 'single nationality state', ethnic Turks faced assimilation campaigns that restricted their linguistic, educational, and religious rights (after the Bulgarian communist regime had expelled a quarter of a million Turks in the early 1950s). Popular anti-Russian feeling remained strong in Poland, Hungary, and Romania—each of which had fought against Soviet Russia in the recent past. Both Poland and Hungary had witnessed uprisings against the Soviet-backed and Soviet-imposed communist political systems in 1956, and Romanian attitudes towards the USSR were coloured by the Soviet annexation of Bessarabia and Northern Bukovina in 1940.

As in the west, in central and eastern Europe relations with Germany were key to constructing a stable postwar order. This meant reconciliation between Poland and Germany. Following its shift to the west and its absorption of the 'recovered territories'—that is, most of the formerly German regions of Silesia, Pomerania, and East Prussia—postwar Poland emerged fearful of a German resurgence. The concern was mitigated somewhat by the creation of the GDR, which recognized the Oder–Neisse frontier in July 1950 and served as something of a buffer state between the FRG and Poland. Nevertheless, the fear of German revanchism remained. After Władislaw Gomułka (Minister for the Recovered Territories from 1945 to 1948 and de facto leader of the country until 1948, when he was removed for 'rightist-nationalist deviation') re-emerged to become head of the ruling Polish United Workers' Party, he sought to allay Soviet anxiety about Polish 'anti-Soviet' sentiment by informing Khrushchev in October 1956: 'Poland needs friendship with the Soviet Union more than the Soviet Union needs friendship with Poland.... Without the Soviet Union we cannot maintain our borders with the West.' Postwar West Germany's decades-long unwillingness to recognize the Oder–Neisse frontier helped to keep Poland embedded within the framework of the Soviet bloc.

That unwillingness to accept the territorial losses that had followed defeat remained for a generation. Kurt Schumacher (who emerged as the leader of the Social Democrats in the western occupation zones and the early FRG) expressed what many Germans felt when he declared in October 1945: 'Germany will never recognize that Oder–Neisse-Line as determined by the four victorious powers in Potsdam as the German border.' The millions of Germans who had lost their former homes in the east formed a potential reservoir of irredentist politics. Associations of uprooted Silesians, Pomeranians, and East Prussians gained substantial membership in West Germany during the 1950s and 1960s, and the 'Association of Expellees and those Deprived of Rights' attracted notable if short-lived electoral support. Their hope to return to their former

'Heimat' was unrealistic, however. In Cold War Europe there was no scope for restoring German sovereignty over regions that the postwar FRG regarded as temporarily 'under Polish administration'. It took a generation before the reality of Germany's postwar borders was accepted, when the Social–Liberal coalition government headed by Willy Brandt signed the Warsaw Treaty of 7 December 1970. (The FRG formally recognized the Oder–Neisse frontier when the country was unified in 1990.)

Scarcely less remarkable, but much less remarked upon, was the postwar recognition by Poland of the country's *eastern* border, with Ukraine. With the end of the Second World War and the westward expansion of the USSR, the postwar Polish government consented to the loss of western Ukraine and Belarus—territories that Poland had ruled at various times over the centuries and that were included in independent Poland after the First World War—that became part of the Soviet Union. Like the postwar Polish–German border, the postwar Polish–Ukrainian border remained accepted after the end of the Cold War.

It was with the Final Act of the Conference on Security and Cooperation in Europe, agreed at Helsinki in the summer of 1975, that the states of Europe (with the exception of Albania, but including Iceland, Canada, and the USA) confirmed the inviolability of their frontiers and thus finally acknowledged the postwar map of Europe. In a sense the Helsinki Final Act, and with it the acceptance of the postwar equilibrium in Europe, seemed to mark the end—or at least the beginning of the end—of the postwar era. Yet this equilibrium was short-lived, ending less than two decades later as a consequence of the collapse of the USSR and the Soviet bloc.

In the years leading up to the collapse of Soviet-style communism in Europe, nationalist sentiment gained in potency in the eastern half of the continent. During its final years in the 1980s the Soviet Union witnessed a growing emphasis on 'Russianness'; the GDR came increasingly to endorse its 'German' aspects and venerate Frederick the Great; and patriotism rather than socialism increasingly was used to mobilize support in the 'people's republics'. Whereas the prospect of building a new socialist order had inspired many Europeans after the Second World War, by the 1980s pseudo-Marxist platitudes fell on increasingly deaf ears and nationalism was grasped as a means to underpin political legitimacy.

Nationalism was particularly potent in the Balkans. Yugoslavia and Albania had drawn on nationalist sentiments to maintain distance from the Soviet Union during the Cold War, and their conflicting nationalisms fuelled friction between them (fanned by the fact that the great majority of the population of Kosovo in the Yugoslav Federation were ethnic Albanians). After 1945 the Yugoslav government under Josip Broz Tito (the son of a Croatian father and a Slovenian mother in a state where Serbs formed the largest ethnic group) suppressed manifestations of nationalism, to prevent any of the federation's nationalities from becoming politically dominant. The combination of political independence, hostility from Stalin's USSR during the postwar schism, Tito's prestige, some economic successes, and freedom to travel and to live and work abroad (most notably in West Germany, which contained more than half a million Yugoslav labour migrants in 1973) lent the state a measure of popular support. However, after Tito's death in 1980 this arrangement crumbled as the multi-ethnic society fell apart, and was followed in the 1990s by bloody wars and the break-up of the Yugoslav federation in 1992.

While tensions never exploded in postwar Czechoslovakia, friction remained between the Czech half of the state and Slovakia; and the end of the communist straitjacket was followed by the 'Velvet Divorce' and Slovak independence in January 1993. For Hungary, which had lost two-thirds of its territory following the First World War and failed to regain the lost territories after being on the losing side in the Second, the national question continued to fester:

in postwar Europe some three million ethnic Hungarians found themselves in Czechoslovakia, Ukraine, Yugoslavia, and Romania.

Within the USSR, national identity was never completely replaced through socialist ideology, and when the Soviet Union dissolved, nationalist sentiment provided much of the solvent. In the Baltic republics of Estonia, Latvia, and Lithuania, resentment over the extinguishing of national independence during the Second World War, the influx of Russians after 1945, and deportations to Siberia during Stalin's rule rose to the surface once Mikhail Gorbachev's policy of *glasnost* lifted the lid on dissent. Public demonstrations began in all three Baltic republics in 1987, and were followed by the formation of independence movements that scored striking electoral victories in 1989. In August 1989 roughly 1.8 million people formed a 650-kilometre-long human chain from Vilnius through Riga to Tallinn, affirming identities separate from the USSR. Emboldened national movements pushed for independence: in October 1990 the Latvian Popular Front announced that it would aim for complete independence; in December 1990 the majority of the Lithuanian Communist Party declared in favour of independence—a move followed by Gorbachev's attempt to reverse this by force; and in March 1991 Boris Yeltsin (Chairman of the Russian Supreme Soviet from May 1990) signed an agreement of mutual recognition of sovereignty between Russia and the Baltic republics. A 'genuine and widespread national renaissance' (Tony Judt) across the Baltic states helped to end the supra-national project of the USSR and with it the political structure of postwar Europe.

More important to the Soviet Union as a *union* was Ukraine. Not only had the 13th-century Kievan 'Rus' been regarded by Russian nationalists as central to the formation of Russian identity, but Ukraine had occupied an important role in the integrated economy and politics of the USSR. Yet its recent history also revealed centrifugal forces, with the assertion and then loss of Ukrainian independence after the First World War and continued resistance to Soviet rule in the early postwar years. In addition, population changes during and after the Second World War—the murder of much of Ukraine's Jewish population, the annexation of eastern Galicia and western Volhynia, and the expulsion of their Polish population—made Ukraine much more 'Ukrainian'. The weakening of the USSR in the late 1980s was paralleled by growing Ukrainian national consciousness, particularly in western Ukraine. In July 1990 the Ukrainian Soviet voted in favour of Ukrainian sovereignty, and in August 1991 Ukraine's parliament declared the country's full independence—a decision approved by over 90 per cent of the population in a referendum in December 1991.

Two further European Soviet republics that became independent states were Belarus and Moldova (Byelorussia and Moldavia in their Soviet iterations). Belarus' independence was not a consequence of anti-Russian sentiment, but more an opportunist response to the collapse of the USSR; its declaration of sovereignty came in July 1990, just two weeks after that step had been taken in Ukraine. Soviet Moldavia—which had had a short-lived autonomy in the wake of the Bolshevik Revolution and then was incorporated into Romania, annexed by the USSR in 1940, reoccupied by Romania from 1941 to 1944, and after the war again fell to the USSR—declared itself sovereign in June 1990 and declared its independence in August 1991. Moldovan independence was followed by the breaking away (and military conflict lasting from November 1990 to July 1993) of a narrow strip of land bordering Ukraine to form 'Transnistria', a state not recognized internationally, but whose existence was supported by Russia.

With the splitting off of one former Soviet republic after another, the failure to organize a viable community of post-Soviet sovereign states, and Boris Yeltsin's success in bringing economic and financial affairs in Russian territory under *Russian* control, by late 1991 not much remained of the Soviet Union. After the leaders of Russia, Ukraine, and Belarus met on 8 December and declared that 'the USSR had ceased to exist', there was little left for Gorbachev but to resign as Soviet President.

By the time the Soviet Union dissolved, the socialist regimes of eastern Europe were no more. The dissolution of the socialist bloc had begun a decade earlier with the creation of the independent trade union *Solidarność* (Solidarity) in Poland in August 1980 (to which the Polish government responded with the imposition of martial law). During the 1980s eastern Europe's socialist regimes faced mounting economic difficulties, inability to initiate meaningful reform, disintegrating ideological commitment, popular discontent, and a growing sense of national identity. Their system had been hollowed out, and it was only a matter of time before the socialist house of cards would collapse.

At the centre of the transformation was Germany. Like their counterparts elsewhere in socialist eastern Europe, during the 1980s the GDR and its geriatric political leadership found themselves confronted by economic stagnation and smouldering discontent that had been kept in check by a pervasive police apparatus. The dam broke in autumn 1989, in the wake of the 40th anniversary of the founding of the east German state and the visit of Gorbachev. Protest demonstrations grew in size and number, and once the GDR leadership backed away from adopting the 'Chinese solution' of violently crushing the protests their regime crumbled, culminating in the breaching of the Berlin Wall on 9 November. Despite initial hopes that a reformed, democratic east German state might survive, the process of German reunification—essentially of the incorporation of the GDR into the FRG—rapidly ensued. With the end of the GDR and the reunification of Germany on 3 October 1990, the division at the centre of Europe dissolved.

Key to this epoch-ending earthquake was the unwillingness of the Soviet leadership to call in the tanks as they had done in the 1950s and 1960s. Without this backing and facing popular unrest, eastern Europe's socialist dictatorships collapsed one after another: in August 1989 the independent trade union *Solidarność* was invited to form a government in Poland; on 23 October 1989 the Hungarian People's Republic was abolished and the Republic of Hungary proclaimed; in November 1989 the Czechoslovak Communist Party gave up power after being confronted by mass protest and a general strike, and in December Gustáv Husák resigned as Czechoslovak President; in December 1989 communist rule in Romania came to a bloody end, and its leader Nicolae Ceauşescu was executed on Christmas Day. By the time Lech Wałęsa was elected Poland's President in December 1990, Europe's postwar geopolitical order, structured around the continent's political division, was no more.

In western Europe domestic unrest did not produce such fundamental challenges, but it did surface. The UK experienced considerable industrial conflict in the 1970s and 1980s, culminating in the miners' strike of 1984–5. More damaging were the Northern Ireland 'Troubles', which erupted in the wake of the Catholic civil-rights movement in the late 1960s. The violence involving Catholic paramilitary groups seeking Irish unification, Protestant paramilitary groups seeking to maintain Northern Ireland's place within the UK, and the British Army, which was deployed on Northern Ireland's streets, claimed the lives of some 3,500 people between 1969 and the signing of the Good Friday Agreement in 1998.

On the European continent nationalist movements challenged the centralized states of France and Spain. Postwar France had to contend with Breton nationalist agitation, Corsican separatism, and nationalism among its Basque population along the Spanish border. In Spain, the Franco regime (which sought to suppress separatist movements in the Basque country, Catalunya, and Galicia, and the public use of the Basque and Catalan languages) and its successors had to contend with violent Basque nationalism. In December 1973 the underground paramilitary formation ETA

(*Euzkadi Ta Askatasuna*, Basque Homeland and Freedom)
succeeded in assassinating Franco's Prime Minister Admiral Luis
Carrero Blanco, and was responsible for numerous other terrorist
attacks which killed or injured hundreds of people. Nationalist
sentiment grew in Catalunya and in Galicia as well.

Despite undercurrents of divisive nationalism and eruptions of
conflict, and after the tumultuous history of the previous decades,
the political history of postwar western Europe was generally
characterized by relative stability. During the 1950s only France
experienced something approaching regime change, with the
demise of the Fourth Republic and its replacement in 1958 by the
Fifth, but that ended with de Gaulle's return to stabilize French
politics. The Belgian political system emerged intact through the
royal crisis of 1950 provoked by the contentious return and then
abdication in short order of King Leopold III. The British political
system weathered the Suez crisis of 1956, when British foreign
policy suffered a catastrophic setback and Prime Minister Anthony
Eden had to step down. And the Italian and West German political
systems overcame terrorist challenges in the 1970s without their
political systems collapsing or opting for authoritarian rule. In
contrast to what had happened in Europe after the First World
War, postwar western European democratic states demonstrated
impressive levels of legitimacy and resilience.

The remarkable success of relatively consensual democratic
politics in western Europe was something that (except perhaps in
the Scandinavian countries and the UK) had been hardly a
foregone conclusion in 1945. Alongside the reconciliation of
conservatism to democratic government, the formation of this new
political landscape was made possible by the transition of left-wing
parties and trade unions from class-struggle politics towards a
model aimed at extending the welfare state. This was signalled by
the abandonment by the Social Democratic Party of Germany of its
Marxist heritage in favour of becoming a broad *Volkspartei*
('people's party') with the *Godesberg Programm* of 1959, by the

eclipse of the French PCF by France's Socialist Party during the 1970s and 1980s, and by the jettisoning by the Spanish Socialist Party of its Marxist ideology in 1979. Their political successes came not as movements of the industrial working class, but by drawing support from across the social spectrum and, increasingly, from people who worked in the expanding public sector.

This transition allowed social-democratic parties effectively to challenge conservative parties that had dominated hitherto. In the UK, the Labour Party's electoral victories (narrowly) in 1964 and (substantially) in 1966 ended more than a dozen years of Conservative government. In West Germany, when the social–liberal coalition came to power in 1969 (with the Social Democrat Willy Brandt promising to 'dare more democracy'), for the first time since the FRG was founded its Chancellor was not a Christian Democrat. In Austria the Social Democrats (led from 1967 by Bruno Kreisky) emerged in the 1970 general election as the largest party, able to form a minority government; in 1971 it won an absolute majority, after which the Social Democrats dominated Austrian politics for a decade. In France the long march of the reformist French left brought veteran politician François Mitterrand to the Élysée Palace in May 1981 as the first socialist President of the Fifth Republic. And in Spain the election victory of the Socialist Party under Felipe González in 1982 ushered in a period of social-democratic government that lasted for the next 14 years. The path charted by Scandinavian Social Democrats appeared to be the path to success, at least until economic and political troubles eroded the basis of social-democratic liberalism and Keynesian economics.

Whereas support for communist parties in western Europe generally waned—most sharply in West Germany, later and less precipitously in France and Spain (but not in Italy, where the PCI's share of the popular vote rose from roughly a quarter in 1963 to more than a third in 1976)—a new challenge arose in the shape of an upsurge of left-wing radicalism among the postwar generation.

Yet only a minority of this generation were involved or even necessarily supported their contemporaries protesting on the streets of Paris and elsewhere, and the noisy 'anti-authoritarian' politics of the student protesters of '1968' and their allies soon were pushed back. The belief that 'the worldwide wave of protests, rallies, marches, sit-ins, and battles with the police ... brought consternation to the capitalist establishment of the West and the bureaucratic establishment of the deformed workers' states of the East [and] hope and inspiration to truly revolutionary socialist forces everywhere' was largely disappointed. '1968' may have evoked visions of a utopian, anti-authoritarian future, but its lasting resonance was more in the cultural sphere than in the realms of politics, economic policy, or international affairs. The conditions for the free-ranging radicalism of the 1960s quickly evaporated. Instead, from the 1970s onwards radical politics, at least in western Europe, focused more on gender equality (with the rise of feminist movements), environmental concerns and protection (with the growth of Green parties), and multiculturalism (with the growing numbers of immigrants from beyond Europe and their—often contested—integration in the political system).

While the dreams of '1968' soon faded, those of European integration were more durable. Underpinned by the 'idea of Europe' that transcended the divisions and conflicts of nation-states, western European integration was one of the great projects of the postwar era. This was carried forward in the Maastricht Treaty—the Founding Treaty of the European Union—which was signed by the 12 members of the EC in 1992 and came into effect in 1993. Designed to extend the Treaty of Rome that had brought about the creation of the EEC in 1957, the Maastricht Treaty looked towards economic and monetary union and envisaged a common citizenship. Driven by Jacques Delors (President of the European Commission, 1985–95), it envisaged a deeper, more integrated Europe—just as the geopolitical order that had framed postwar Europe was washed away as the continent's Cold War division disintegrated.

When the Second World War ended, it seemed unlikely that half a century later one might be able to speak of a triumph of democracy on the European continent. Yet at the dawn of the new millennium that appeared to have happened. In western Europe the political challenges of overcoming the terrible legacy of the war had been met successfully. Former socialist dictatorships had transitioned into parliamentary democracies and opted for the 'west'. And the authoritarian regimes of the Iberian peninsula—those of Antonio de Oliveira Salazar in Portugal and Francisco Franco in Spain, both of which dated from before the Second World War and maintained dictatorial rule for decades after 1945—crumbled during the 1970s. (Portugal's *Estado Novo* collapsed in the 'Carnation Revolution' of 1974 after having been undermined by colonial wars in Angola and Mozambique. In Spain Franco's death in 1975 was followed by free elections in 1977, a new democratic constitution in 1978, a failed coup attempted by disgruntled militarists in 1981, and a landslide victory of the Socialist Party in 1982. In January 1986 both Spain and Portugal were able to enter the western European mainstream as democratic states and join the EC.)

At the end of the millennium Europe's political landscape appeared remarkably benign: European conservatism had accepted democratic politics; radical right-wing political movements had largely been relegated to the margins; the southern tier of Europe's authoritarian governments had left the stage; Soviet-style state socialism had collapsed; left-wing parties across western Europe had jettisoned class-conflict politics in favour of spreading the benefits of the welfare state across society; the economic problems and unrest that surfaced during the 1970s had ebbed; European integration appeared to be moving ahead; war on the continent seemed almost unimaginable.

As younger generations—the post-postwar generations for whom the postwar era was past history rather than lived experience—came of age, there appeared ample grounds for an optimism that

Europe had emerged from the shadows of the Second World War and its immediate aftermath. One could look back and regard the triumph of parliamentary democracy as the unlikely outcome of the war. However, with the upsurge of authoritarianism, xenophobia, and war in more recent years, the optimism that once framed European postwar political history has dissipated. The postwar era in European politics may have come to an end with the dawn of the new millennium, but history had not.

Chapter 8
The end of empire and its consequences

On 8 May 1945, the day after the act of military surrender was signed by German officers at SHAEF headquarters in Reims, a parade to celebrate Germany's capitulation descended into violence when French gendarmes tried to seize banners opposing colonial rule in Sétif in north-eastern Algeria (then considered an integral part of France). An anti-French riot followed, and the French gendarmerie fired on the march of some 5,000 Muslims demanding an end to French rule. The clashes in Sétif (and similar police repression, on a somewhat smaller scale, in nearby Guelma) were followed by attacks on French settlers (*colons* or *pieds-noirs*) in the surrounding countryside; the French colonial military and police forces responded with reprisals and summary executions, while *pieds-noirs* vigilantes lynched Muslims taken from local jails and shot Muslims not wearing white armbands as they had been instructed to do by the army. Altogether the violence left thousands of Arabs—estimates vary from 6,000 to 30,000, with Algerians claiming as many as 45,000—as well as roughly 100 French settlers dead.

The violence at Sétif and Guelma did not resonate greatly among the French public during the immediate aftermath. Not until the outbreak of France's war in Algeria in November 1954 did the conflict in North Africa occupy a central place in French politics and public life. However, the Sétif massacre marked what has been termed 'a fundamental step in the creation of an Algerian nation'. The formal end of the Second World War in Europe occurred at the same moment as the beginning of postwar colonial wars that would continue for more than three decades (Figure 11).

11. A stamp printed in Algeria dedicated to the 30th anniversary of the violence in Sétif, Guelma, and Kherrata on the day of the end of the Second World War in Europe.

Loss of empire is a central theme in the history of 20th-century Europe. In the wake of the First World War its land empires collapsed, with the demise of the Habsburgs, the Hohenzollerns, the Romanovs, and the Ottomans. With their defeat in the Second World War, Fascist Italy and Nazi Germany lost their empires. After the Second World War it was the turn of western European powers to see their maritime empires crumble (leaving the USSR with a land empire that expanded in the wake of the war).

When the Second World War formally ended in Europe in 1945, the British, French, Dutch, Belgians, Spanish, and Portuguese still had overseas colonies. (Italy had to surrender its African colonies—Libya, Eritrea, Somalia—immediately after the war; the formal end of the defunct Italian empire came with the Treaty of Peace with Italy—one of the Paris Peace Treaties—in 1947.) Western Europe's colonial powers faced the challenge of reasserting control over their overseas territories with diminished resources, a challenge compounded for the Dutch, the French, and the Belgians as they were emerging from German occupation themselves. Where European colonies had been seized during the war—for instance from the French in Indochina, from the Dutch in the East Indies, from the British in Malaya and Hong Kong—their former rulers in effect would need to recolonize them. At the same time, overseas colonies assumed heightened economic importance for weakened European imperial powers, not least as sources of primary products that could be sold for sorely needed hard currency.

After the Second World War the Dutch found themselves in a particularly weak position. The Royal Dutch East Indies Armies had surrendered to the Japanese in Java in March 1942, and two days after Emperor Hirohito announced the Japanese surrender on 15 August 1945 the nationalist leaders Sukarno and Mohammad Hatta declared an independent Republic of Indonesia. While the Dutch faced a mammoth task of reconstruction at home, they sought to reimpose colonial rule on the other side of the world. A four-and-a-half-year-long military campaign followed: Dutch forces (with British and Australian support in 1945 and 1946) fought an anti-guerrilla recolonization war that included numerous 'pacification' campaigns, 'police actions', and massacres of the civilian population. Altogether the Netherlands deployed more than 200,000 troops to suppress the insurgency, over 160,000 of whom were Dutch (the rest recruited locally). By the time the conflict ended and the Netherlands recognized the Indonesian Republic in December 1949, roughly 5,000 Dutch men had died, as had a vastly greater number of Indonesians.

France made even greater, more protracted, and ultimately no more successful efforts to resurrect empire. The restoration of imperial links was regarded as necessary for France's economic and political recovery. According to Gaston Monnerville, the Chairman of France's Consultative Assembly, in May 1945, 'without the Empire, France would be merely a liberated country. Thanks to her Empire, France counts amongst the victors.' However, with the 1946 Constitution of the Fourth Republic, France and its empire formally became a single entity, the French Union (*Union française*). No longer did France have 'colonies', but rather 'overseas departments' (*départements d'outre mer*—e.g. Martinique, Guadeloupe, Réunion), 'overseas territories' (*territoires d'outre mer*, e.g the colonies in sub-Saharan Africa and the Pacific, as well as Madagascar), and 'associated states' (e.g. Tunisia, Morocco, and the territories in Indochina), while Algeria remained as three *départements* of the French Republic. Yet new labels did not create new realities: rights of citizenship were not necessarily enjoyed by all the inhabitants of overseas territories, and anything viewed as 'insurrection' was met with 'the full colonial treatment'.

Among the first to receive 'the full colonial treatment' were inhabitants of Madagascar, where French forces were deployed in 1947 to crush a nationalist revolt. What followed was a campaign of collective terror against people supposedly hiding rebels, the burning of entire villages, torture, and executions, resulting in the deaths of roughly 550 Europeans and 90,000 natives of Madagascar. This was the least remembered of France's bloody campaigns to crush independence movements in its overseas territories. More significant, in terms of both loss of life and impact on politics, were the wars that the French fought and lost in Indochina and Algeria.

With the Japanese defeat in 1945, France's provisional government sought to reinstate colonial rule in Indochina. However, on 2 September 1945—the same day that Japan formally surrendered to the Americans on the USS *Missouri*—Hồ Chí Minh proclaimed Vietnam's independence. After a short-lived incursion by the (Nationalist) Chinese in the north of Vietnam and British intervention in the south, the French returned to overthrow Hồ Chí Minh's government. An insurgency followed, beginning in December 1946 and developing into full-scale war. Altogether over half a million soldiers fought on France's behalf, most of whom were from the French Union (largely from Algeria, Morocco, Tunisia, and Senegal, as well as within Indochina) and the French Foreign Legion, alongside a minority who were professional soldiers from metropolitan France.

Nevertheless, and despite substantial military and financial aid from the United States, the attempt to resurrect French rule in Indochina was doomed to failure, and by 1954 only a tiny minority of the French public favoured continuing the military campaign. The war continued until the French were defeated at iện Biên Phủ in March–May 1954 and the government (led by the Radical politician Pierre Mendès-France, who had long opposed French colonialism and the war in Indochina) agreed at the International Geneva Conference of July 1954 to hand over Vietnam north of the 17th parallel to the Việt Minh. (This left the south ruled by the Emperor Bảo ại, who would be removed a year later by his Prime Minister, Ngô ình Diệm.) By the time the war ended, the French had lost over 100,000 soldiers, of whom roughly 20,000 were

French, while the great majority came from African French Union territories or Indochina itself; between 175,000 and 300,000 Việt Minh soldiers also died or were missing, with estimates ranging as high as 400,000.

France's colonial war in Indochina divided public opinion and contributed to the instability of the Fourth Republic. (During the course of the Indochina War there had been 17 different governments in Paris.) It provoked a widely supported antiwar movement (spearheaded by the communists) among the French; and in 1956 the loss of Indochina was attributed by General Henri Navarre, who had been in overall command of French forces at the time of iện Biên Phủ, to politicians who had 'allowed the army to be stabbed in the back'. Nevertheless, the long-term effects of the Indochina war on French society and politics were limited: Indochina had not seen significant French colonial settlement; the French had not sent conscripts to fight there, using professional soldiers and volunteers instead; and the Indochina conflict was followed by another colonial war, involving many more French soldiers and many more French casualties, in a country closer to France and with a large French settler population: Algeria.

Whereas the failed colonial enterprise in Indochina could be regarded as peripheral to metropolitan France, and while the French felt able to grant independence to Morocco and Tunisia in 1956, the liberation struggle that erupted in Algeria in November 1954, barely six months after iện Biên Phủ, was a different matter. Algeria was administratively part of France, and its European settler population—roughly a million people, or about one-tenth of the population—regarded Algeria as France, not a colony. Indeed, the city of Algiers had been a part of France longer than had Nice; and Algeria's second city, Oran, had twice as many *pieds-noirs* inhabitants as Muslims.

This framed French understandings of the struggle in Algeria. In 1954 François Mitterrand, then French Interior Minister, passionately supported military action in Algeria, telling the *Assemblée nationale*: 'Algeria is France. And who amongst you, *Mesdames* and *messieurs*, would hesitate to employ all methods to preserve France?' And in 1955 Premier Mendès-France, who had overseen France's exit from Indochina, declared to the *Assemblée nationale*: 'One does not compromise when it comes to defending the internal peace of the nation, the unity and integrity of the Republic.'

France's campaign to crush the revolt of the *Front de libération nationale* (FLN, established by Ahmed Ben Bella in 1954) was described as 'police operations', 'actions to maintain order', 'operations to restore civil peace', and 'peacekeeping operations'. French 'police operations', and the campaign of the FLN for Algerian independence, quickly became a spiral of violence and reprisal, shootings and bombings, massacres and summary executions. A state of emergency was declared in 1955; military rule replaced civilian rule; and by the summer of 1957 French troop levels in Algeria had reached 450,000. At its peak, the war was fought on the streets of Algiers for much of 1957 as the French military employed emergency powers (and torture), effectively sidelining the civil administration. The French military leadership was determined to prevent a repeat of the humiliation suffered in Indochina: according to General Raoul Salan, the French commander-in-chief during the Battle of Algiers, the role of France's soldiers in Algeria 'would be to protect these French *départements* from Indochina's fate and maintain the integrity of national territory'.

However, not only did they fail to protect Algeria 'from Indochina's fate' or to 'maintain the integrity of national territory' (if by 'national territory' one included Algeria), they also precipitated the end of the Fourth Republic and nearly destroyed France's postwar democratic system. When Generals Jacques Massu (who had led French forces in the Battle of Algiers) and Raoul Salan, alarmed that the government in Paris would reach an agreement with the

FLN to end the conflict and faced with mob violence and rioting by settlers in Algeria, established a 'Committee of Public Safety' in Algiers in 1958, essentially they were staging a coup—calling for a Government of Public Safety in Paris to be led by Charles de Gaulle.

De Gaulle agreed to emerge from political retirement and assume leadership of the Republic, provided that a new constitution be introduced built around a powerful presidency. Yet the conflict did not end until France conceded Algerian independence in July 1962. Opponents of the war urged military insubordination; the FLN found support among the 350,000-strong Algerian population resident in France; French police and military personnel were targeted for assassination; the Algerian migrant community within France was terrorized by police (culminating in the massacre of as many as 200 Algerians demonstrating in Paris on 17 October 1961); and the *Organisation de l'armée secrète* (OAS, formed in 1960 of military figures involved in the 1958 coup attempt and members of the French settler community) mounted a last-ditch terror campaign to prevent Algerian independence, a campaign that claimed thousands of lives in Algeria and France, and in August 1962 nearly managed to assassinate de Gaulle.

In the event, it was left to de Gaulle to extricate France from the Algerian (and colonial) quagmire and to save its political system. Before Algeria became independent in 1962, over 25,000 French soldiers had died and another 65,000 been wounded; more than 140,000 FLN fighters had been killed, along with tens of thousands of Muslim civilians. Something approaching a million European-Algerians (*pieds-noirs*) subsequently fled the country that they had called their home, as did roughly 90,000 *Harkis*—Muslim Algerians who had served as auxiliaries in the French army. Among the *pieds-noirs* who fled were over 150,000 Jews; together with North African Jews who left other newly independent countries, they would change the composition of the Jewish community in postwar France.

(Algerian independence also led to the first exit of a country from what later became the EU. Algeria, which as constitutionally part of France had been a member of the EEC from 1957 to 1962, discontinued its membership after becoming independent. The second to exit was Greenland, which left the EEC in 1985, following a referendum in 1982.)

Elsewhere France's overseas possessions achieved independence more peacefully, with the wave of decolonization across Africa carried out in 1960 under de Gaulle's presidency. However, the processes of decolonization in sub-Saharan Africa were not without pressure on newly independent francophone states to remain within the French sphere of influence.

Following the failed Dutch and French campaigns against anti-colonial insurgencies, Belgium had little desire to follow a similar path. Nevertheless, when Africans in the Belgian Congo demonstrated in 1959 for independence and rioting followed in Leopoldville (from 1966, Kinshasa), the colonial military *Force publique* responded with live fire, killing hundreds. The Belgians soon bowed to the inevitable, conceding Congolese independence in June 1960 (followed by the independence of Rwanda and Burundi in 1962). However, their retreat was not followed by a peaceful transition. Instead, there was a mutiny among the Belgian forces, Belgian military intervention to protect their nationals, the precipitous flight of tens of thousands of white settlers, the rise of secessionist movements (most notably with the establishment in July 1960 of a breakaway state in Katanga), intervention by mercenary forces and UN peacekeepers, the removal from office and subsequent murder of the first Prime Minister of the Republic of the Congo, Patrice Lumumba, and years of instability that left hundreds of thousands dead before the country was reunified in 1965 under the rule of General Joseph-Desiré Mobutu (who would remain in power until 1997). Within Belgium, the country's colonial enterprise had been more a project of the country's francophone population than of its Flemish speakers, and after the end of empire, divisions between Flemings and Walloons increasingly occupied centre stage in Belgian politics.

Of the colonial empires dismantled after the Second World War, the largest was the British. Britain emerged from the war in a diminished condition to resist pressures for independence in its colonial possessions. At the same time the UK's economic difficulties gave the Attlee government a strong motivation to reconsolidate the empire, not least to provide export opportunities for earning desperately needed dollars. A major focus was on Malaya, which before the Second World War had been the world's largest supplier of natural rubber, the largest dollar-earning export of the Sterling area, and which consequently was of considerable economic importance to the UK. Faced with large debts to the USA, the postwar Labour government also sought to increase the production of foodstuffs in Britain's colonies in order to reduce dependence on the Americans. (A prime example was the failed postwar scheme to cultivate groundnuts—peanuts—on three million acres in East Africa.)

The greatest immediate challenge was that posed in India, and it was clear to the Labour government from the time it came to power in July 1945 that, as Attlee observed in his memoirs, 'the Indian problem would have to be faced'. The postwar Labour government thus took its first decisive steps towards shedding its empire with the end of colonial rule in India in 1947, as hopes that India might somehow remain within the imperial frame crumbled in the face of popular demands for independence and spiralling communal violence between Hindus and Muslims. The British government wanted to leave India quickly and acceded to the Muslim League's demand for partition, which was followed by an avalanche of bloodshed in which millions of people fled their homes on the 'wrong' side of the lines of partition and roughly one million lost their lives. The hasty exit from India, and the granting of independence to Burma and Ceylon in 1948, signalled a fundamental shift in the UK's place in the postwar world.

Labour was replaced in government by the Conservatives from 1951 to 1964, and the 1950s and 1960s saw the end of British rule over most of what had constituted its empire. In West Africa, where there were no substantial white settler populations, the British had little enthusiasm to stand in the way of independence. Thus the Gold Coast (Ghana) achieved independence peacefully in 1957, Nigeria in 1960, and Sierra Leone in 1961. Elsewhere, however, the British engaged in one counter-insurgency campaign after another in ultimately unsuccessful efforts to forestall decolonization: in Kenya between 1952 and 1956, in Cyprus between 1955 and 1959, in Oman between 1957 and 1960, in Aden between 1963 and 1967, and in Malaya, where over a dozen years British forces overwhelmed the Malayan National Liberation Army, which surrendered in 1960. In Kenya between 1952 and 1960 some 10,000 British soldiers, more than 20,000 police and settler irregulars, as well as Kikuyu 'loyalists', engaged in the campaign to crush the Mau Mau rebellion—a campaign that included the carpet bombing of forests harbouring Mau Mau rebels, the imprisonment of hundreds of thousands of suspected insurgents, the forced resettlement of roughly a million people into 'protected villages', and the hanging of over a thousand rebels. The numbers of Africans killed or who died in the British detention camps has been estimated to be in the tens of thousands; by the time the war ended (and the British proclaimed victory) roughly 20,000 Mau Mau rebels and perhaps 100,000 Kikuyu civilians had died.

Nevertheless, whereas in France the scars left by the Algerian War festered for decades, most of the UK's colonial military campaigns made little lasting impression on the country's public memory. Instead the British congratulated themselves that they were leading the way in granting independence to their colonies. Both Labour and Conservative governments had become aware of the UK's limited ability to hold back what Prime Minister Harold Macmillan famously referred to in Cape Town in February 1960 as the 'winds of change'. The waning attraction of empire was reflected in the decline of the annual celebration of 'Empire Day': by the late 1950s the Conservative government came to recognize that 'Empire Day' no longer carried much meaning, and in December 1958 Macmillan changed its name to 'Commonwealth Day'.

By the mid-1960s there was no longer a question of the UK intervening militarily in its erstwhile colonies. In (Southern) Rhodesia (which became Zimbabwe in 1980) the white-settler government of Ian Smith proclaimed its Unilateral Declaration of Independence (UDI) in November 1965 and resisted Black-majority rule with its own forces. While white-ruled Rhodesia continued to enjoy some support on the political right in Britain, there was no broad appetite for the UK either to support Smith's regime or to intervene to overturn UDI.

It was not insurgencies in Britain's colonies, but the Suez crisis of 1956 that provided a shock to the UK political system. The Suez fiasco plunged the UK into its most serious postwar political crisis: it ended the career of Prime Minister Sir Anthony Eden, split the Conservative Party and British public opinion, and spelled the end of Britain's postwar pretensions to be a great power. However, the UK political system did not face an existential threat. The British soon put the 1956 disaster behind them—a disaster that, in the view of Edward Heath, was instrumental in altering the UK's postwar orientation from the Commonwealth to Europe.

On the Iberian peninsula, both Spain and Portugal faced the loss of their colonies and subsequently saw their future in an integrated Europe rather than in remnants of empire. For Spain this involved territories consolidated in 1946 as Spanish West Africa, and the challenge came from Morocco, which, upon gaining independence from France in 1956, was determined to regain what it regarded as its territory. Following violent demonstrations in April 1957 in the Spanish enclave of Ifni on Morocco's Atlantic coast, the Franco regime sent units of the Spanish Legion to suppress unrest.

Morocco then sent troops to surround Ifni, marking the beginning of the Ifni War. In April 1958 a peace treaty was signed, ceding the Spanish protectorate in southern Morocco, and in July the Moroccan Army of Liberation (not part of the regular Moroccan armed forces) declared a ceasefire. The Spanish (with French help) won the war militarily and held Ifni until 1969, when it returned the territory to Morocco. Spain held Spanish Sahara until 1976, when it withdrew following the Green March of 6 November 1975 (a demonstration involving roughly 350,000 Moroccans who marched into the Western Sahara territory).

Faced with the growing challenge of Basque separatism at home, keen to improve relations with the western democracies, and with Franco increasingly incapacitated by illness—after suffering a heart attack in October 1975, Franco died on 20 November—Spain could not afford to get bogged down in a colonial war in Africa. The Spanish colonial enterprise was over, and Western Sahara was divided between Morocco and Mauritania. The Ifni War has been referred to in Spain as the Forgotten War (*la Guerra Olvidada*), and was excluded from the Spanish school curriculum on Franco's orders. Compared with what happened in other western European colonies, the end of Spain's African colonial domain was a minor affair. It did not result in a mass exodus of European settlers, and it did not shake the Spanish political system (although it did undermine the self-confidence of the Spanish military). Instead, it coincided with the crumbling of the Franco dictatorship, whose days were numbered in any event.

By contrast it was in the last of Europe's colonial powers that the end of empire led to the greatest upheaval at home. Portugal had been the first European country to establish a maritime empire and the last to see it dissolve. Whereas the Dutch, French, Belgians, and British largely divested themselves, or were divested of, their colonial possessions between the end of the Second World War and the 1960s, Portugal's *Estado Novo* regime remained a colonial power into the 1970s. The Portuguese government denied that it was engaged in colonialism; instead, it asserted that its 'overseas provinces' were an 'integral, inseparable part of Portugal' and counted the inhabitants of Portuguese Africa alongside inhabitants of European Portugal as Portuguese citizens.

Although challenges to Portugal's colonial empire came relatively late, during the 1960s nationalist movements arose in Angola (in 1961), Mozambique (in 1964), and Guinea-Bissau (in 1963), and grew into armed rebellions that in the 1970s would overcome Portuguese rule. Like that of the French in Indochina and Algeria, the Dutch in Indonesia, and the British in Kenya, the Portuguese response was brutal and ultimately unsuccessful. Altogether Portugal mobilized over 800,000 soldiers for its colonial wars, of whom more than 8,000 were killed. (African casualties numbered in the hundreds of thousands.) The fact that Portugal's military were overstretched and had no prospect of a satisfactory conclusion, together with the economic burdens created by the counter-insurgency campaigns (which consumed 22 per cent of state expenditure between 1961 and 1974), finally broke the *Estado Novo* regime, which was overthrown in a military coup in April 1974.

The new government quickly abandoned the colonial enterprise, withdrew Portuguese military forces from Africa, and granted independence to Portuguese Guinea (in 1974) and to Angola, Mozambique, Cape Verde, and São Tomé and Principe (in 1975). After a year of political turbulence, a new Portuguese constitution was drafted in 1975, and following elections in 1976 the first constitutional government took office under the leadership of the moderate socialist Mário Suares. Not only had Portugal's colonies been freed of Portuguese rule and Portugal freed of the crippling expense of its counter-insurgency campaigns, but also the Portuguese were freed from the *Estado Novo* dictatorship—a rare case of colonies in effect liberating the colonizers.

The precipitate end of Portugal's colonial empire had profound consequences for Portuguese society, with a mass exodus of

Portuguese citizens from the African territories, mostly from Angola and Mozambique. Between 500,000 and 800,000 largely destitute refugees, settlers, and their dependants—the *retornados*—were brought in haste, often in a state of shock and facing hostility, to Portugal, a relatively poor country whose population at the time was only a little over nine million. This constituted what was, in relative terms, the largest migration that had resulted from decolonization. It also brought conflict to Portugal itself, as some who had come from the military became involved in organizations opposing the democratic transition and in the unrest that rocked the country in 1975.

The end of empire offered Portugal a route out from its peripheral position and opened the door to integration into postwar western Europe. While Portugal's economic shift towards western Europe had already begun during the 1960s and early 1970s, the cutting of colonial ties, the end of dictatorship, and its replacement by democratic government paved the way for membership of the EC in 1986. The Portuguese no longer looked overseas (i.e. to the colonies or to Brazil) to escape poverty at home; they looked instead to more prosperous regions of the EC/EU. The end of empire also changed the sense of Portuguese national identity, leaving the authoritarian and colonialist past behind and looking instead to a democratic 'European destiny'.

The 'return' of the *retornados* (many of whom had been born in the colonies rather than Portugal) was but one element of the migration of Europeans from newly independent former colonies to postwar Europe. Not only European settlers, but also substantial numbers of European civil servants, administrators, officials, and their families returned to their home countries once the lands where they had been employed or stationed became independent. Consequently many civil servants and administrators in postwar western Europe had had experience in the colonies, with careers that had included sudden breaks when those colonies achieved their independence. Others saw their careers cut short—for example, the thousands of British overseas civil servants who faced premature retirement when colonial rule ended. Many found influential administrative positions in postwar Britain—in business, government, or the rapidly expanding higher-education sector (where half a dozen became university Vice-Chancellors).

Altogether, between 1945 and 1985 between 5.4 and 6.8 million people migrated to western Europe from former colonies; of these between 3.3 and 4 million were European or partly so. In a sense, the experiences of the Dutch who left independent Indonesia, the French *pieds-noirs* who left Algeria after independence, and the Portuguese *retornados* paralleled those of Germans uprooted from what had been eastern Germany and of Poles uprooted from what had been eastern Poland at the end of the Second World War. It would take years before those compelled to leave their homes behind would integrate fully into the European societies to which they came.

That, however, was far from the end of the story. Postwar Europe may have retreated from empire, but empire did not retreat from postwar Europe. With the demise of Europe's maritime empires, huge numbers of people from what had been European colonies made their way to Europe. As campaigners against restrictions on Commonwealth immigrants in Britain put it in the 1960s, 'We're here because you were there.' During the early years after independence, many were able to take advantage of legal status that offered them European citizenships. For example, by creating the single status of 'Citizen of the United Kingdom and Colonies', the British Nationality Act of 1948 effectively established equal British citizenship for all colonial and Commonwealth subjects, allowing them freely to migrate to and live and work in Britain. This gave some 800 million people in the Commonwealth the right to claim British citizenship, and thus right of abode in the UK.

France responded similarly to the postwar question of how to classify its colonial subjects, when the French empire became the

French Union in 1946 and a new constitution was ratified that made colonial subjects Union citizens (while Algeria retained its status as three *départements* of France). In the wake of their loss of Indonesia, with the Charter of the Kingdom of the Netherlands introduced in 1954 the Dutch extended the right to live and work in the Netherlands to the inhabitants of Suriname (on the northeast coast of South America) and the Netherlands Antilles; Portugal reclassified its African and Asian colonies as 'overseas provinces' in 1951 and in 1961 granted Portuguese citizenship to their entire populations, regardless of their colour or place of birth. Thus by the beginning of the 1960s hundreds of millions of people who had lived in overseas colonial territories of European powers possessed the right to live and work in Europe.

Hundreds of thousands proceeded to take advantage of the possibilities this presented, during a period of economic expansion and growing employment opportunities. In France, where Poles and Italians had comprised half of the country's foreign population before the Second World War, there was a huge increase in immigration from North Africa, particularly of Algerians. Between 1947 and Algerian independence in 1962, Algerians enjoyed the same freedom to reside in France as did European French citizens; their number in France rose from 211,000 in 1954, at the outset of the Algerian War, to 350,000 when the war ended in 1962. (In 1982 it stood at more than 800,000.) During the 1960s there was also a notable increase in immigration into France from Morocco and Tunisia, after the French government reached agreements with these countries in 1963 to provide needed labour. Although primary migration from outside the EEC was halted in 1974, the numbers of North African immigrants in France continued to climb as a consequence of family reunification, which brought in more women and children and thus changed the composition of immigrant communities. (Migration to France from sub-Saharan Africa picked up only in the 1980s, as a result of political upheaval: the number of Africans from south of the Maghreb in 1975 was roughly 82,000, but it had risen to 158,000 by 1982, to 240,000 in 1990, and to 282,000 in 1999.)

In areas where migrants to France settled in substantial numbers—Paris and its suburbs, which received the largest numbers, and southern cities, most notably Marseille, where the city's Jewish and Muslim populations surged following France's exit from her North African colonies—immigration from the southern side of the Mediterranean changed the face of society. Belleville, a magnet for immigrants in north-east Paris, was described in the 1970s:

> Walking along the Boulevard de Belleville any evening one could be forgiven for thinking it was a North African *souk*. Shops, cafés, cinemas, restaurants and peddlers serve the local immigrant population which is made up mainly of Sephardic Jews and Moslems. Life begins in the side streets and along the boulevard at dusk on Saturday, ending at noon on Friday; Arabic, not French, is the language used in the street, and the only reminder of France is the CRS bus parked permanently outside the entrance to the Belleville metro, the occasional investigation of cafés by posses of police.

Immigration from former colonies changed the face of postwar Britain as well. The emergence of postwar non-white immigration into the UK is often regarded as the arrival from Jamaica of hundreds of West Indians (many of them ex-servicemen) on the former troopship *Empire Windrush* at the Port of Tilbury on 21 June 1948. While they were the most visible non-white immigrants in Britain during the 1950s—by 1960 there were 115,000 West Indians in the UK—they were not the only ones: tens of thousands of immigrants arrived from India and Pakistan (numbering some 55,000 by 1960), and some 25,000 had arrived from West Africa. However, the open door to Commonwealth immigration soon became less open, as restrictions on entry into the UK were introduced with the Commonwealth Immigration Acts of 1962 and 1968 and with further legislation in 1971. Nevertheless, the flow of

Commonwealth and colonial migration increased as people rushed to 'beat the ban', and by 1971 the number of people of South Asian origin in Britain exceeded half a million. The Jamaican-born cultural theorist Stuart Hall observed that 'the very moment Britain convinced itself it had to decolonise, that it had to get rid of its colonies, the colonised began flooding into England'; 'Commonwealth migration, as a permanent legacy of empire, had created a multiracial Britain and religious pluralism.'

In the Netherlands too, postwar migration changed the country. Immigrants came from both the former Dutch East Indies and the West Indies, as well as from Suriname during the 1970s, in an effort to beat restrictions as the Dutch looked to curb migration during a period of economic difficulty. The first great wave of post-colonial immigration into the Netherlands had come from independent Indonesia: between the late 1940s and the early 1960s 300,000 'repatriates' (of whom roughly 180,000 were *Indisch*, i.e. of mixed Indonesian and European descent) came to the Netherlands as Dutch citizens. A special group came from the Moluccas Islands, many of whom had served in the Royal Dutch Indies Army and whose descendants formed a source of discontent that erupted in a series of terrorist outrages in the Netherlands during the 1970s. However, in terms of its effects upon Dutch society, the exodus from Suriname proportionally had the greatest impact, as more than a third of its population (of less than 400,000) left during the 1970s. During the 1980s and 1990s, after migration from Suriname had dwindled, the Netherlands Antilles became a main source of migration to the Netherlands; more recently, however, their numbers were exceeded by foreign workers from Turkey and Morocco and their descendants.

In Portugal, which during the 1960s and early 1970s had been a source of migrant labour elsewhere in Europe (most notably France), immigration from among once-colonized peoples (from the Cape Verde Islands, Angola, Mozambique, Guinea-Bissau, São Tomé and Principe, and Goa) accelerated as its empire disintegrated. The end of empire and the political revolution of 1974 transformed Portugal into a target for immigration as well as a source of emigration. This also precipitated a more restrictive immigration policy and nationality law, which in 1975 largely limited citizenship to people with Portuguese ancestry. Thus people who had once been allowed to enter and settle in Portugal legally became foreigners present in the country illegally.

The experience of Belgium was rather different, in that most of its post-colonial immigration did not originate in its own empire. After its colonial rule ended, most of Belgium's non-European migrants did not come from the Congo (or Zaïre, as it was called between 1971 and 1997). Whereas nearly a tenth of Belgium's population of roughly 10 million were foreign-born in 1991, the country's non-Europeans came largely from Turkey and Morocco. The Congolese comprised only a small proportion of non-European migration into Belgium (often settling in the increasingly multicultural municipality of Ixelles in Brussels); and while their numbers increased in the 1990s, migrants from the Congo tended more to go to France than to Belgium.

Altogether, millions of people made the journey from the colonies or—in even greater numbers—from newly independent states, to western Europe, bringing with them their cultures, faiths, and tastes. European societies had always been multicultural and shaped by migration, but the postwar migration into (western) Europe was different in that so much of it came from beyond Europe's shores.

Immigration from Europe's former colonies changed the sights and smells of many towns and neighbourhoods in postwar (western) Europe, from Manchester's 'Curry Mile' (Wilmslow Road in Rusholme) and Southall ('Little Punjab') in suburban West London to Belleville in the north-east of Paris (home to many North Africans from the 1960s and to Chinese from the 1980s) to Ixelles in Brussels (with its large Congolese population). European diets altered, with the increased availability of ingredients used in non-European cuisines; thousands of 'ethnic' restaurants, opened by immigrants from Europe's erstwhile colonies, changed European eating habits. In April 2001, the British Foreign Secretary Robin Cook illustrated his optimism about the future of Britain and Britishness by asserting that 'Chicken Tikka Masala is now the true British national dish, not only because it is the most popular, but because it is a perfect illustration of the way Britain absorbs and adapts external influences.' One might have described the spread of Indonesian cuisine in the Netherlands or the popularity of North African cuisine in France in a similar manner.

However, post-colonial immigration into Europe was reflected not just in Europeans adapting and absorbing external influences as they consumed curries or couscous, or took holidays on the beaches of Bali, Sri Lanka, Jamaica, or Goa. It was also reflected in the growth of support for populist anti-immigrant politics, particularly from the 1970s onwards as economic difficulties coincided with increased non-European immigration into western Europe. The most prominent of Europe's populist movements that grew during this period was the *Front national* (since 2018 the *Rassemblement national*) in France. Founded by Jean-Marie Le Pen in 1972, the programme of the *Front national* featured Euroscepticism, protectionism, and, increasingly, opposition to non-European immigration deemed to threaten French identity. The *Front national* saw some electoral success in the 1980s, winning 10 of France's seats in the European Parliament in 1984 and with Jean-Marie Le Pen managing to attract 14.4 per cent of the votes in the first round of the 1988 presidential election. A similar development occurred in Flemish-speaking Belgium, where the *Vlaams Blok* (formed as an electoral alliance between the Flemish National Party and the Flemish People's Party in 1978 and as a party in its own right in 1979) achieved success. By focusing during the late 1980s on immigration, the *Vlaams Blok* more than trebled its popular vote between the general elections of 1987 and 1991.

Immigration also figured in postwar British politics. In the 1964 general election, the Conservative Peter Griffiths unseated Labour's Patrick Gordon Walker in Smethwick in an ugly campaign in which Griffiths's supporters employed the slogan, 'If you want a nigger for a neighbour, vote Labour.' In April 1968 in Birmingham the Conservative MP Enoch Powell opposed Commonwealth immigration in a famously provocative lecture, which became known as the 'rivers of blood speech' and brought him considerable popular support as well as widespread public condemnation and dismissal from the Shadow Cabinet by Conservative Party leader Edward Heath. In a television interview in January 1978 Margaret Thatcher, then leader of the opposition, won attention when she stated that the British people feared they 'might be rather swamped by people with a different culture'. Fraser Nelson observed: 'She killed the National Front that night, as voters who were concerned about immigration believed they had, in her, someone who understood them.' In contrast to its continental counterparts, the National Front remained on the fringes of British politics; instead of an expected electoral breakthrough it did miserably in the 1979 general election, winning only 0.6 per cent of the vote.

Although postwar Europe's interactions with the non-European world primarily involved states whose maritime empires disintegrated after the Second World War, their resonance was wider. European countries that no longer were, or never really had been, colonial powers also were affected. In Austria, which had had no overseas colonies, the Freedom Party (*Freiheitliche Partei Österreichs*) emerged from the fringes of politics with a shift to anti-immigration politics once Jörg Haider became its leader in 1986 against a background of a rapid increase in the country's Muslim population. And in Denmark the influence of anti-immigration parties (the Progress Party—*Fremskridtspartiet*—and the Danish People's Party—*Dansk Folkeparti*) increased from the 1980s with their opposition to the integration of 'non-Western immigrants'.

While they had been neither colonial powers nor magnets for migrants, postwar eastern European states were not unaffected by contact with the 'Third World'. Europe's socialist states brought students from developing countries to study in their educational institutions and provided (relatively small amounts of) military aid as expressions of 'anti-imperialist solidarity'. Poland, for example, offered 'Lumumba Scholarships' for university study, and the GDR supplied military advisers in Ethiopia as well as military equipment to SWAPO in Namibia for its struggle against South Africa. Nevertheless, non-Europeans constituted only a minuscule proportion of the populations of postwar eastern European countries, and non-white faces remained a comparative rarity on their streets—something that continued to provide a striking contrast between western and eastern Europe after the collapse of the Soviet Union and its allied socialist regimes.

One may view postwar Europe as a collection of collapsing empires—beginning perhaps with the defeat of Italy (and the liquidation of its empire) and Germany (whose Second World War had been a war of imperial conquest), extending through the collapse of the Dutch, French, British, Belgian, Spanish, and Portuguese empires, and then followed by the crumbling of the Soviet empire in 1989–91. It is possible to regard the idea of a postwar Europe set on the path of peaceful economic and political integration as a substitute for its lost empires. Yet while the European continent itself was relatively peaceful from the 1950s until the outbreak of war in Yugoslavia, the transition from empire was anything but peaceful. The dismantling of European empires and colonialism after the Second World War involved waves of violence that can only be described as war crimes, despite justifications at the time. The end of Europe's empires was accompanied and enabled by war, by wars that European imperial powers lost. In the process, postwar Europe developed both new ideas about itself and new social, cultural, and political realities. Postwar Europe was Europe after empire.

Chapter 9
Postwar cultures

In the decades after the Second World War, Europe's cultural landscapes reflected many of the transformations that reshaped postwar European society. In the first instance, however, cultural institutions needed to recover from the enormous damage left by the conflict. In meeting this challenge they revived remarkably swiftly, to reassert the continent's cultural heritage and to help create what many hoped would be a new and better world.

The determination to reassert the importance of cultural life could be seen in the rapid reopening of museums, concert halls, and theatres. Museums had suffered greatly as a result of war. Collections had been evacuated, split up, or looted, and many museum buildings had been damaged or destroyed. Yet in Warsaw, for example, Poland's National Museum, which had been used to garrison Germans soldiers during the war and whose collections had been systemically looted, was re-established as the war-torn country's central museum already on 7 May 1945 and began to receive 'restitution shipments' during the following month. The world's two largest museums, the Louvre in Paris and the Hermitage in Leningrad, also managed to reopen quickly; much of their collections had been evacuated before war had come and were returned to the museums soon after the conflict ended. The same was true for the National Gallery in London, as part of its collection was returned from Wales, and already on 17 May 1945 an exhibition of paintings opened in the east wing of the Gallery at Trafalgar Square.

European orchestras also made remarkable efforts to welcome audiences again. The Berlin Philharmonic, which had lost two successive venues to bombing, continued its concerts during the early postwar years in a converted cinema; later, in 1963, the new *Philharmonie*, designed by Hans Scharoun, opened in West Berlin. Leipzig's *Gewandhausorchester* had lost its Concert House to bombing in 1943, but from 1945 it was performing again, first in a music hall, then in a cinema, and later in the city's Congress Hall before moving to the freshly built New Opera House in 1960. The La Scala opera house in Milan, heavily damaged in 1943, was hastily repaired and reopened in May 1946 with a concert conducted by Arturo Toscanini. In Warsaw, where the old Philharmonic Hall had been destroyed (and roughly half of the orchestra's musicians had died) during the war, the Philharmonic reopened for the 1947/8 season and was able to move into a new, modern Philharmonic Hall upon its completion in 1955.

The revival of theatre was equally rapid. On 27 May 1945, only three and a half weeks after the German capitulation, the first postwar theatre première took place in Berlin; between June and December 1945 more than 120 premières were staged in theatres, community halls, school auditoriums, and cinemas in the shattered German capital. The Polish capital's Grand Theatre (the home of Polish National Opera and the Polish National Ballet), which had been bombed and almost completely destroyed during the war, was restored and expanded at great expense after 1945; when the rebuilt 1,800-seat theatre opened in 1965 it was among the largest in the world.

Cultural revival in the wake of war was not just about resuscitating the old; it was also about embracing the new. In painting, sculpture, and architecture, modernism, which had its roots well before 1945 and had spread in response to the First World War, triumphed in the wake of the Second. The 1950s saw the establishment of numerous galleries and art exhibitions displaying modern art, notably the *Dokumenta* in Kassel (founded by Arnold Bode in 1955, with the aim of reconnecting Germany with the international art world through a 'presentation of twentieth-century art'). Cultural figures associated with modernism achieved prominence across postwar western Europe. Among the most notable were the sculptor Henry Moore, who won the International Sculpture Prize at the Venice Biennale in 1948 and whose works were placed in prominent public locations (e.g. the 'reclining figures' on the South Bank in London for the 1951 Festival of Britain and at the UNESCO building in Paris in 1958, and the 'family group' created for Harlow New Town in 1954); and the architect Le Corbusier (Charles-Édouard Jeanneret-Gris), whose postwar commissions included the Chapelle Notre-Dame-du-Haut de Ronchamp (completed in 1955) and the massive apartment blocks termed *Unité d'habitation*, the first of which was built in Marseilles between 1947 and 1952, the second in Nantes between 1950 and 1955, and the third in West Berlin between 1956 and 1958.

After the war entire urban districts were rebuilt in the modern style. One of the largest projects was the reconstruction of the French port of Le Havre, which Allied bombing had devastated in 1944: there the architect Auguste Perret, a pioneer in the use of reinforced concrete, designed a new administrative, commercial, and cultural centre of the city—described recently by UNESCO as 'a landmark of the integration of urban planning traditions and a pioneer implementation of modern development in architecture, technology and town planning'. Other prominent examples include the *Grindelhochhäuser* (Grindel High Rises), an ensemble of 12 high-rise apartment blocks constructed in a bombed-out district of Hamburg between 1946 and 1956; the 1957 International Building Exhibition (INTERBAU) in West Berlin with the *Hansaviertel* project, which included a series of modernist high-rise apartment houses; and the centre of Rotterdam, which had been flattened by bombing in May 1940 and which was to be a beautiful modern 'city of twentieth-century people' with 'the speeding traffic, the broad boulevards, all the tall buildings [that] will generate a sense of bustle that blends harmoniously with modern life'.

The modernist idiom also entered another arena of postwar European culture: the home. From the 1950s, the staid furnishings of earlier decades were increasingly replaced by modern 'organic' forms using new materials, including plastics. This organic design became increasingly popular across the west: in Scandinavia, Italy, France, and in West Germany, where the 'economic miracle' years saw *Nierentisch* modernism enter the domestic environment in the form of lamps, furniture, tables, etc., and symbolize a fresh start in the new postwar world. (The opportunities offered by colourful plastic products were also grasped in the GDR, where Walther Ulbricht referred to them as 'an essential element of the socialist cultural revolution'.) 'Danish Modern' furniture design, which had its origins in the 1920s, flourished in the two decades after the Second World War as mass-production techniques propelled a thriving furniture industry. In Britain Terence Conran opened the first Habitat store in Chelsea, in London, in 1964. Perhaps the greatest transformative influence on the domestic-furnishing culture of postwar Europe came from Ingvar Kamprad's IKEA, which began selling furniture by mail order in 1948, opened its first store in Sweden in 1958 (followed by Norway in 1963, Denmark in 1969, Switzerland in 1973, and West Germany in 1974), brought modern(ist) European design into millions of homes, and eventually became the world's largest furniture retailer.

The attraction of the modern(ist) vision reached its peak in the 1960s and began to fade towards the end of that decade and in the 1970s, when it increasingly fell out of favour. If the postwar period saw the apogee of modernism, its end seems to have coincided (at least in the west) with the turn towards postmodernism from the early 1980s.

On the eastern side of the political divide, postwar cultural fashion was initially framed less by modernism (the innovations seen in the Soviet Union during the 1920s having been jettisoned) than by Socialist Realism, alongside neoclassicism in its representative architecture. The formula of the early (Stalinist) postwar years was 'socialist in content, national in form'. Yet the *Zhdanovshchina* (after Andrei Zhdanov, Stalin's cultural theorist and proponent of Socialist Realism, which remained official Communist Party policy until 1956) left little room for diversity. Instead, cultural expressions stifled uncomfortable themes, while reflecting the triumph of socialism in monumental building projects (such as the 237-metre-tall Palace of Culture in Warsaw, completed in 1955; the skyscraper of the Latvian Academy of Sciences in Riga, built between 1951 and 1961; and East Berlin's grand socialist boulevard, the Stalinallee, built between 1951 and 1960 and renamed the Karl-Marx-Allee in 1961). From the 1960s onwards, however, building projects in the eastern bloc adopted the modernist international style. By the 1980s it had become difficult to distinguish housing projects in eastern Europe from their western European counterparts.

An important driver of cultural production in postwar Europe was government patronage and subsidy. A prominent example was the Arts Council of Great Britain, founded in 1946, but with its origins in the wartime 'Council for the Encouragement of Music and the Arts' established in 1940, whose first chairman was John Maynard Keynes (until his death in 1946). The Arts Council became a major sponsor, supporting the creative and performing arts, commissioning art works for the 1951 Festival of Britain, and establishing a network of cultural organizations across the country under the Labour government of 1964 to 1970. In France, once President de Gaulle named the novelist André Malraux as Minister of Cultural Affairs (a post he held from 1958 until 1969), large-scale state funding for the arts spread across the country, not least through the creation of *maisons de la culture* in provincial cities. In the FRG, massive government expenditure supported the restoration and rebuilding of theatres, concert halls, opera houses, and museums.

The socialist states of postwar eastern Europe also generously subsidized cultural institutions. Support was provided for theatres, libraries, museums, orchestras, and opera companies. Remarkably cheap tickets to performances of classical music and drama were offered to the public, with seats often being provided through trade unions. Cultural institutions and producers were supported well— as long as they stayed in line; and while many artists and intellectuals were silenced or went into exile, those who remained acquiescent benefited from the state's largesse.

Underpinning the consumption of culture in postwar Europe was growth in real incomes. Together with the achievement of a five-day working week, which became more common from the second half of the 1950s onwards, this gave many western Europeans, including those in working-class households, time and money to spend on leisure pursuits. (The citizens of socialist eastern Europe lagged behind in this regard.) During the 1950s and 1960s increasing amounts of increasing incomes were spent on entertainment, travel, enjoyment, and popular arts.

Entertainment and cultural products entered private homes in growing measure, as the proportion of households with record players, radios, and televisions grew rapidly. In Great Britain, the lowest social strata doubled their expenditure on entertainment and vacations between 1954 and 1971. In England four out of five families possessed a television in 1965; in the FRG this level was achieved five years later, and in France it was reached in the mid-1970s. (A similar trend unfolded to the east: in the Soviet Union, only about one million households possessed a television set in 1955, but this rose to ten million by 1963 and to roughly 25 million by the end of the 1960s.) This signalled a significant shift in cultural consumption as people were now spending 15–20 hours per week on average in front of the box. Television broadcasting—

by state-run or public-service broadcasting organizations—expanded, in both the numbers of channels available and the hours of programming offered. The continued growth of radio ownership—more than 90 per cent of households in both the FRG and Britain possessed at least one radio by 1955—and of record players brought new musical tastes and pop culture not simply into homes, but into the bedrooms of western Europe's teenagers.

Although visits to the cinema fell as television viewing rose during the postwar years—in Britain 1948 marked the high point of ticket sales for the cinema and by 1960 the number had declined by two-thirds, and in the FRG the number of visits to the cinema halved between 1956 and 1964—film remained an important element of mass popular culture.

Postwar European cinema had lost important figures who fled Germany and Austria before the war for careers in the New World (e.g. Billy Wilder, Peter Lorre, Marlene Dietrich, Fritz Lang, and Hedy Lamarr). Nevertheless, after 1945 European cinema developed in new directions, and European film festivals were launched in Cannes, Karlovy Vary, and Locarno (1946), Edinburgh (1947), Berlin (1951), and London (1957). In Italy, a group of film directors then in their forties (notably Vittorio de Sica, born in 1901, and Roberto Rossellini and Luchino Visconti, both born in 1906) committed themselves to a new cinema of *Neorealismo* (neorealism), filming on location rather than in studios, often using non-professional actors, aiming to address the difficulties of life in the early postwar years. Although hardly a commercial success and fading by the 1950s—of the films made in Italy between 1945 and 1953 only about a tenth were neorealist, most of which did not succeed at the box office—Italian neorealism influenced others, notably the French *Nouvelle Vague* (New Wave), which emerged in the late 1950s and early 1960s and was identified with directors Jean-Luc Godard, François Truffaut, Éric Röhmer, and Claude Chabrol.

Britain saw its own New Wave at roughly the same time, associated particularly with the films of Tony Richardson. In West Germany the *Neuer Deutscher Film* (New German Cinema) was influenced by the *Nouvelle Vague*, coming to prominence in the 1960s and early 1980s, with Rainer Werner Fassbinder, Werner Herzog, and Volker Schlöndorff among its directors. To the east was the *Polska Szkoła Filmowa* (Polish Film School) of the late 1950s and early 1960s (whose most prominent director was Andrzej Wajda), which was influenced by the Italian neorealists and which in turn influenced the Czechoslovak New Wave of the 1960s (whose directors included Miloš Forman and Jiří Menzel). Many of the critically acclaimed films coming from these movements dealt with the war and its legacy: Rossellini's *Rome, Open City*; Wajda's *Ashes and Diamonds*; Menzel's *Closely Watched Trains*; Schlöndorff's *The Tin Drum*; and Fassbinder's *The Marriage of Maria Braun*.

Popular culture in postwar Europe was influenced massively by the USA. Of course, American influences were not completely new to Europe after 1945: on the eve of the Second World War Clark Gable had been among the most popular film actors in Nazi Germany, and when Coca-Cola opened bottling plants in western European countries in the late 1940s, its arrival in West Germany in 1949 was heralded with the slogan *Coca Cola ist wieder da* ('Coca Cola is here again'). However, what occurred after the Second World War was of a different magnitude. American films played in (western) European cinemas; American music, from jazz to swing and rock 'n' roll, filled the air; American products proved attractive in a Europe emerging from wartime deprivation and postwar austerity. The presence of American troops in western Europe—most famously Elvis Presley, who was stationed in Germany between October 1958 and March 1960, and who had an enormous influence on the tastes of young Europeans in the late 1950s—and the broadcasts by the American Forces Network (AFN) brought American pop music and rock 'n' roll to tens of millions of Europeans (on both sides of the Iron Curtain).

American postwar cultural advance was not without its critics, as 'Americanization' was perceived not just as a promise, but also as a threat. Anti-Americanism as a cultural phenomenon in Europe pre-dated the Second World War, and became a widespread feature of postwar European experience. During the late 1940s in France, for example, there was reaction against 'Coca-Colonization' and, more sharply, against the *Civilisation atlantique* that was bitterly caricatured in the 1953 painting of that name by the communist artist André Fourgeron (Figure 12). In West Germany, where the United States had seemed an attractive alternative to a conservative political culture, the enthusiasm with which President Kennedy was greeted in the early 1960s evaporated with the US escalation of the Vietnam War; and during the 1960s and 1970s criticism of consumerism and 'McDonaldization' grew among German intellectuals, environmentalists, and peace groups alongside aversion to the presence of the American military.

12. Painting titled *Atlantic Civilisation* by Andre Fourgeron, dated 1953.

The advent of postwar 'youth culture' was not simply a matter of American imports. During the late 1950s and early 1960s western Europe had its own pop music idols: Freddy Quinn (born Franz Eugen Helmut Manfred Nidl) was 'THE superstar in the Fifties and Sixties' in West Germany and Austria; and France had its rock star in Johnny Hallyday (born Jean-Philippe Smet). However, it was in Britain that homegrown popular music really took off, with a generation of musicians born during the war who experienced their childhood in the late 1940s and 1950s, and who were in their twenties when they conquered the charts in the 1960s: The Beatles (with John Lennon, born in 1940, and Paul McCartney, born in 1942), The Rolling Stones (with Mick Jagger and Keith Richards, both born in 1943, and Brian Jones, born in 1942), and The Who (whose lead guitarist Pete Townshend, who wrote the song 'My Generation', was born in May 1945).

This postwar cultural shift reflected the postwar generation coming of age, during a time of increasing affluence. From the late 1950s young (western) Europeans increasingly had money of their own to spend on themselves. They bought their own clothes in styles distinctive of youth, from jeans to mini-skirts—as Tony Judt observed, 'they *looked* different'. They bought their own music in the form of gramophone records; they viewed American films, which offered images of the prosperous consumer society and 'the American way of life'; they watched television, which during the 1950s and 1960s was in more and more people's homes. And more and more young western Europeans gained an understanding of English.

Western pop culture also seeped into the eastern half of the continent and aroused the ire of socialist rulers determined to limit its influence. During Stalin's last years harsh criticism was aimed at jazz, 'melancholy tangos and vulgar foxtrots', and what Soviet Deputy Prime Minister Georgii Malenkov termed in 1950 'jazz-style dance music'. During the second half of the 1950s the new expression of western youth culture, rock 'n' roll, provoked official disapproval. Emanating from the USA, it was denigrated (e.g. in 1956 in the GDR) as 'nonculture' that appealed to primitive human beings (*Urmenschen*). (The GDR comprised something of a special case, as western pop music was easily available through AFN, and before the Berlin Wall was constructed in August 1961 many young people regularly crossed into West Berlin to see films, frequent music halls, and buy records as well as blue jeans.)

From the 1960s onwards, the cultural straitjacket loosened intermittently in socialist eastern Europe. Homegrown rock bands formed—such as the Puhdys, the flagship band for East German rock formed in the late 1960s, and the Hungarian rock bands Illés, formed in 1960, and Omega, formed in 1962 and described as 'the most successful rock band in Hungarian history'. Yet they could not match the attraction of the music from the west—revealed sensationally on 7 October 1969, the 20th anniversary of the founding of the GDR, when thousands gathered near the Berlin Wall following rumours that The Rolling Stones were to give a concert from the roof of the Springer building (overlooking the Wall on the western side), leading to police intervention and hundreds of arrests. Eastern European regimes had built their Soviet-style Palaces of Culture and celebrated the cultures of the fraternal socialist countries, but their younger citizens were attracted more to the pop culture of the capitalist west than to the socialist virtues trumpeted by their own states.

The growing affluence of postwar Europe brought further cultural influences with the increase in leisure time and (foreign) holidays. Although vacation tourism had begun to spread beyond the well-off upper and upper-middle classes before 1939, what occurred following the Second World War was new—thanks to paid vacations (of increasing length) and rising disposable incomes, improved transport links, and the easing of border and exchange controls. In France, for example, during the 1950s and 1960s a growing number of companies granted their employees four weeks' paid vacation per year, and in 1969 the government legislated four weeks of paid vacation for all; whereas before the war only between 5 and 10 per cent of the French had gone on vacation, by the 1980s more than three-fifths were enjoying summer vacations on the beach, in the countryside, or in second homes.

European tourism became more international, as during the 1960s the growth of package holidays allowed millions of Europeans to enjoy foreign vacations. In West Germany in 1960 just under a tenth of the population travelled to another country on holiday, but by 1966 the figure was 20 per cent and two years later for the first time there were more foreign than domestic vacation trips. Postwar children experienced family holidays, and later travelled as young adults to new locations. Horizons were broadened, as (western) Europeans were exposed to the cultures of other countries, not least to their food cultures; it was in the postwar world that Germans learned to eat spaghetti.

In eastern Europe too vacations gradually became available to larger proportions of the working population. The offerings were more limited than in the west; subsidized holidays were often organized through trade unions; and the possibilities for foreign travel were restricted. Nevertheless, in the socialist half of the continent postwar generations also saw possibilities expand, and during the 1960s and 1970s tourism infrastructure in the socialist bloc expanded to cater for foreign visitors—first from fraternal socialist countries and later from the west (in order to gain hard currency). On the beaches of the Black Sea, as on the beaches of the Mediterranean, more and more Europeans could enjoy their new leisure.

What would perhaps prove to be the most important shift in the cultures of postwar Europe concerned the place of women in society. In the immediate aftermath of the Second World War women had finally gained equal political rights across the continent (e.g. in France in 1944, in Italy in 1945, in Yugoslavia in 1947, in Belgium in 1948); gender equality was inscribed in new constitutions in France (1946), Italy (1947), and the FRG (with the Basic Law of 1949); and in socialist eastern Europe gender equality was part of official state ideology (not least to encourage women to take paid work outside the home). Subsequently, increasing prosperity and the spread of domestic appliances (not least of washing machines) allowed many women to enter postwar consumer culture as 'Mrs Consumer' and 'the new housewife'.

From the 1960s, what has been described as 'second wave feminism', focusing on effective equality beyond the formal achievement of equal rights, gained increasing resonance in western Europe: with the growth of women's organizations, widening access to contraception, campaigns for the legalization of abortion, the establishment of shelters for women escaping domestic violence, and the spread of a feminist press. (In West Germany alone more than 400 feminist periodicals were established between 1973 and 1980.) This coincided with a softening of attitudes towards sex outside marriage (and the removal of legal sanctions on unmarried couples) and what has been termed the sexual revolution.

Western Europe also saw the emergence of important cultural figures whose work and public profiles highlighted women's issues—beginning with Simone de Beauvoir, whose book *Le Deuxième Sexe* (first published in 1949) is one of the foundational texts of modern feminism, and including the writers Doris Lessing and Germaine Greer (both of whom were born outside Europe and came to prominence in the UK), as well as the Portuguese-British visual artist Paula Rego and the German journalist Alice Schwarzer.

Underpinning much of the cultural change in postwar Europe was the changing place of religion in the lives of Europeans after 1945. In the aftermath of the war, Christian religious culture emerged with renewed strength. West Germany, for example, saw something of a religious revival after the demise of National

Socialism, with the clergy enjoying considerable influence, Catholic processions filling the streets, Marian visions attracting hundreds of thousands of pilgrims, and a conviction on both sides of the confessional divide that it was necessary and possible to create a new social order on the basis of a 're-Christianization' of society. In 1954 and 1955 Billy Graham's Christian Crusades enjoyed astounding success, as hundreds of thousands came to hear the American evangelist and filled London's Wembley Stadium, Glasgow's Hampden Park Stadium, and Berlin's Olympic Stadium, as well as venues in Amsterdam, Copenhagen, Geneva, Oslo, and elsewhere. In the political realm, the remarkable success of Christian Democratic parties that emerged after the war might be regarded in part as a consequence of this postwar 'reconfessionalization'.

However, after the early upsurge in popular Christian religiosity, organized Christianity was confronted by the challenge of secularization. Reaction among Catholics to liturgical reforms introduced with the Second Vatican Council of 1962–5—reforms that altered long-standing devotional practices—and cultural liberalization generally undermined ecclesial authority and loosened the social grip of church organizations. The attempt to reconcile church dogma to modern life angered traditionalists while failing to stem the decline in religious practice. Postwar generations became less committed to religious institutions, in what was described in West Germany as a 'silent defection' of many Christians from their faith. In the UK there was an unprecedented rapid decline in Christian religiosity, as the institutional social and cultural bonds of the Christian churches withered following the initial 'return to piety' between the end of the war and the late 1950s, leading *The Times* to assert in November 1989 that Britain was among the 'most godless nations in the Western World'. (It might be noted, however, that this was not the case for Britain's Muslim population: between 1965 and 1985 the number of mosques registered in Britain rose from 13 to 338.)

Similar trends unfolded in the Netherlands, where churches saw decreasing memberships. In Spain, whereas in 1960 over 90 per cent of the population had been self-declared practising Catholics, in 1984 the proportion was only about one-third. In once socially conservative Ireland the decline in the influence of the Catholic Church accelerated towards the end of the 20th century, to create what has been described as a 'post-Catholic Ireland'. In Italy, where in the mid-1950s over two-thirds of Italians regularly attended Mass on Sunday, the government legalized divorce in 1970 and abortion in 1978. As the distance from the Second World War grew, the hold of organized Christian religion on postwar Europeans' lives declined.

While western European countries saw something of a faith revival just after the Second World War, eastern European socialist states, guided by an atheist political philosophy, aimed to suppress public manifestations of religious cultures. Church buildings were taken over for secular purposes; the public role of clergy was severely limited; bookshops (as in the USSR) had sections on atheism rather than religion. Religious instruction in schools was abolished (e.g. in Hungary); churches were destroyed (e.g. in the GDR under Ulbricht, who sought to create a *Gesellschaft ohne Türme*—a society without [church] towers); and secular ceremonies were created as substitutes for religious ones (e.g. the socialist coming-of-age ceremony, the *Jugendweihe*, introduced in the GDR in 1954 as a substitute for church confirmation). (In the GDR this campaign was not without success: between 1949 and 1989 nominal church affiliation among the population fell from 82 to 31 per cent, and by the late 1980s only a tiny proportion of the population were participating actively in traditional religious activities.)

Heads of the Catholic Church who opposed the communist regimes—Cardinal József Mindszenty in Hungary and Cardinal Stefan Wyszyński in Poland—were imprisoned: Wyszyński between 1953 and 1956; Mindszenty from 1948 until 1956, when he was freed in the course of the Hungarian Revolution and subsequently sought refuge in the American Embassy in Budapest, where he lived for the next 15 years. Yet in neither country was the communist regime able to suppress Catholic religiosity. In Poland in particular, the Catholic Church provided an alternative source of authority, culminating in the election in 1978 of Wyszyński's protégé Karol Wojtyła as Pope John Paul II.

The most extreme attempt to suppress religion occurred in Albania, where the majority of the population are Sunni Muslims. There the regime of Enver Hoxha outlawed public religious practice, proclaimed that Albania was an atheist state (complete with a National Museum of Atheism), and criminalized 'religious propaganda'. However, after Hoxha's death in 1985 the regime modified its anti-religious stance, and in 1990 the ban on religious observance was lifted.

Among the most profound changes in the religious cultures of postwar Europe were those brought about by the absence of the millions of European Jews murdered during the Second World War and the presence of millions of Muslims who made Europe their home, especially from the 1970s onwards. With the slaughter of most of eastern Europe's Jews (and the emigration of hundreds of thousands more, especially to Israel) came the eradication of the Jewish cultural centres that had once flourished there, from Vilnius and Kaunas to Warsaw and Lviv. Jewish/Yiddish cultural institutions—synagogues, yeshivas, libraries, theatres, museums, and publishing houses—were lost, and with them much of the Yiddish-language religious culture of eastern Europe. To the west, murder and emigration deprived German-speaking central Europe of many of its most important artists, authors, and musicians, making postwar cultural life in cities such as Vienna and Berlin much the poorer.

After the war, the only major European country where the number of Jews was larger than it had been before the conflict was the UK (some 450,000 as opposed to 300,000 in 1933, but back down to 300,000 in 1988), while in France it was almost as large (235,000 as opposed to 250,000 in 1933). In central and eastern Europe only a fraction remained. Nevertheless, despite their relatively small numbers, Jews continued to play a prominent role in cultural life after the war—for instance in Britain (Isaiah Berlin, George Weidenfeld, Ernst Gombrich, Lucian Freud, Isaac Deutscher, Norbert Elias), France (Raymond Aron, Claude Lévi-Strauss, Sacha Distel), Germany (Marcel Reich-Ranicki, Hans Mayer, Norbert Elias), and Italy (Carlo Levi, Primo Levi).

The contribution of Muslims to the cultures of postwar Europe followed a different trajectory. As a consequence of the rapid growth of Muslim populations in western Europe, particularly from the 1970s, mosques came to form an increasingly prominent feature of the religious architectural landscape of European cities, *halal* foods increasingly became available in restaurants and food shops, and the dress of people in immigrant districts of many large European cities reflected the faith and heritage of their immigrant Muslim populations. The cultures of western Europe's urban centres in particular—music cultures, food cultures, literary cultures (with the rise of post-colonial literature), as well as religious cultures—came to reflect multicultural populations that included large numbers of people from former European colonies and their children.

By the late 1980s, Europe's cultural landscapes were very different from those that existed when the Second Word War ended. Postwar generations had shaped the cultural landscape, as they shaped postwar politics. Prominent postwar cultural figures whose careers had begun either before or soon after the Second World War were leaving the scene—among them the Austrian conductor of the Berlin Philharmonic Herbert von Karajan (born in 1908), who died in July 1989 (just a few months before the Berlin Wall fell); Pablo Picasso (born in 1881), who had died in 1973; Henry Moore (born in 1898), who died in 1986; Jean-Paul Sartre (born in

1905), who died in 1980; Simone de Beauvoir (born in 1908), who died in 1986; Michel Foucault (born 1926), who died in 1984; Samuel Beckett (born 1906), who died in December 1989; and the Nobel Prize winning author (for literature, in 1965) Mikhail Sholokhov (born 1905), who died in 1984. Increasingly, cultural life in Europe would be shaped by people who came from beyond Europe's shores, and who were of neither the wartime nor even postwar generations. After more than four decades, the Second World War receded as a reference point for cultural expression, as Europe entered what had become a post-postwar era.

Chapter 10
When did the postwar era end?

When did the postwar era end? The answer depends on how one conceives of the postwar era, for different approaches lead to different ends of the story.

If the focus is on the immediate military consequences of the war and the demobilization of the soldiers who fought the war in Europe, then one might look to the late 1940s.

If the attention is on Europeans' experiences of daily life, then the end of the postwar period may be located during the 1950s, when the extreme hardships of the war and the immediate postwar years were past and people could settle back into what they regarded as normal rhythms: leaving scarcity behind, enjoying regular employment, establishing a household, moving into an adequate dwelling, acquiring consumer goods beyond the bare necessities.

If the approach concentrates on politics, then the end of the postwar era may be sought either in the stabilization of European political systems by the 1960s, or in the shaking of these systems with the challenges of the late 1960s and 1970s, or in the collapse of eastern European socialism at the end of the 1980s and the reunification of Germany in 1990, or the crumbling of the postwar liberal world order during the early years of the new millennium.

If the answer is framed in terms of international relations, then the end of the postwar era in Europe may be seen in the collapse of the USSR and of the Soviet bloc in 1989–91. Or one might see the meeting between the Marxist Mikhail Gorbachev and the Polish Pope John Paul II at the Vatican in December 1989 as the moment that signalled when Europe's postwar politics had changed fundamentally.

If the focus is primarily on economic development, then the end of the postwar era may be understood as when the postwar economic boom, the *trente glorieuses*, hit the buffers in the early 1970s. It is also possible to see the turning point in the 1980s, when one might believe that the postwar economic settlement was dismantled under the impact of the policies of Margaret Thatcher and Ronald Reagan.

If the response were to centre on (western) Europe's relationship with erstwhile colonies, then one might focus on the end of European colonialism that largely had been completed by the late 1970s.

Or (taking a rather British-centric view) one might even concur with Peter Hennessy, who suggested that the funeral of Queen Elizabeth II on 18 September 2022 marked 'the end of the post-war era'.

The subject also may be approached in terms of generations. This suggests that the end of the postwar era occurred as those who had lived through the war and their children (who had been confronted with the experience of the war through their parents and who comprised the postwar generations) passed from the scene or retired.

In just about all the perspectives outlined above, the experiences of people as members of specific generations play an important role. The political and military figures who shaped the postwar world were of the generations that had experienced the world wars—the First and then the Second—and this shaped how they understood and responded to the challenges they faced. Acceptance of postwar borders, and the fading of expellees' hopes to 'return' to their former homes, came with the passing of the generations that had once lived there and their replacement by younger cohorts that had not. The postwar economic recovery and the expansion of the welfare stare, and how these stalled in the 1970s, were shaped by the demography of the wartime and postwar generations. The transformation of many (western) European societies was affected by both the generations that experienced the anti-colonial struggles of the postwar decades and those who migrated from former colonies to live in Europe. European popular cultures during the postwar decades were expressions of generational consciousness. Then by the early 21st century the formative experiences of the cohorts that had experienced the Second World War had largely ceased to colour European societies and cultures.

The postwar period was not only an era of the emergence of Europe from the extreme violence of the Second World War and its immediate aftermath; it was also an era of absence. The dead of the Second World War were the missing of the postwar era, a presence in their absence. Tens of millions of Europeans lost parents, children, husbands, wives, friends, and those who survived would live with this absence until they themselves died. Viewed in this way, the postwar era came to an end as this absence faded away, when the people who had experienced these losses themselves left the scene.

Concluding her exploration of the commemoration of the massacre at Oradour-sur-Glane in June 1944, Sarah Farmer wrote, shortly before the end of the 20th century:

> As events of the Second World War recede, public memory of the period is becoming more and more independent of individual recollection. Until now, historians of the Second World War have been held accountable in their work by people—individuals and associations—who lived through the events they write about. By the turn of the century, most of the survivors of Oradour will be gone.

A quarter of a century later the survivors of Oradour, together with almost all those who had experienced the Second World War at first hand, are gone. As one 14-year-old Dutch boy responded in the spring of 2018 to a questionnaire about commemoration of the Second World War: 'The war is too far from me. Me and nobody in my family has experienced something during that time.' Once the postwar era reached its end, commemoration had taken the place of memory.

Nevertheless, memories of the Second World War live on and continue to affect the present. Concluding his introduction to *The Oxford Handbook of Postwar European History*, Dan Stone has written:

> When one examines the 'return of memories' that could not be articulated in the public sphere during the Cold War—when the anti-fascist narrative was imposed on the East and prevailed in the West, albeit in a conservative, anti-communist form—one can see that the years since 1989 are intimately connected to World War II and its aftermath. In many ways, we are only now living through the postwar period.

In the decade since Stone offered this assessment, in some ways the war has seemed closer rather than further away. As I have been writing this text, Russia's war against Ukraine has overturned comfortable assumptions about the postwar period as one during which major military conflict between states in Europe was a thing of the past. At the same time, justifications of Russia's invasion, the assertion that Russian forces have been engaged in a crusade against 'Nazis' and for the 'denazification' of Ukraine, overtly draw upon mythologies about the Second World War. Even now, eight decades after the end of the Second World War, the postwar era in Europe may not be completely past.

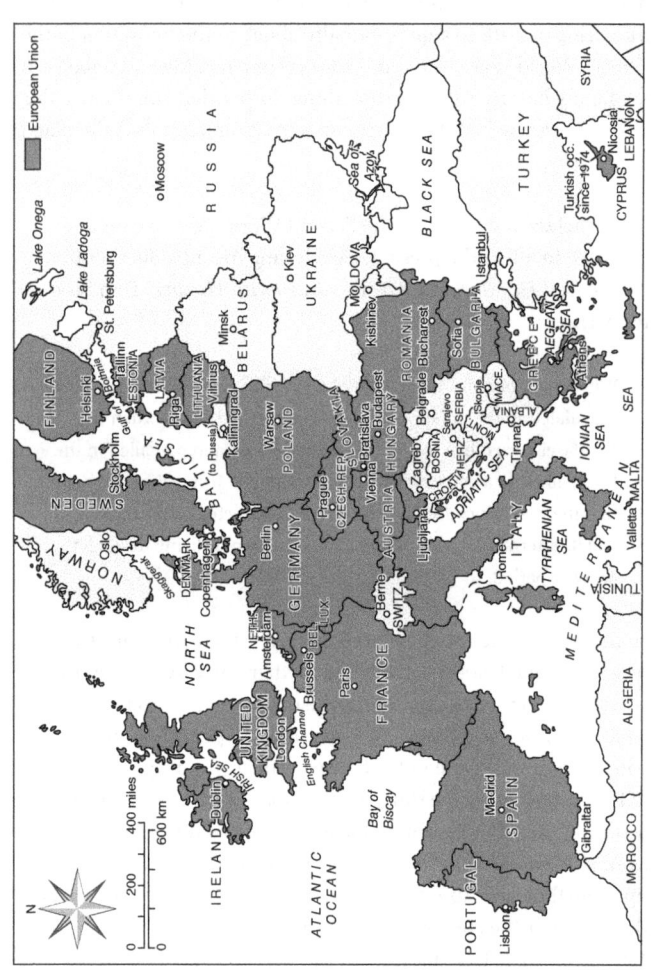

Map 2. Europe in 2012.

References

Chapter 1: What was postwar Europe?

'Seven decades after the end of the second world war on European soil, the Europe we have built since then is under attack': Timothy Garton Ash, 'Why we must not let Europe break apart', *The Guardian*, 9 May 2019.

'Postwar in Europe lasted a very long time, but it is finally coming to a close': Tony Judt, *Postwar: A History of Europe since 1945* (London, 2005), p. 10.

'silence over Europe's recent past was the necessary condition for the construction of a European future': Tony Judt, *Postwar: A History of Europe since 1945* (London, 2005), pp. 8, 10, 61.

Chapter 2: The end of the Second World War in Europe

'On the day of peace I remember my mother ...': 'Fredsdagen minns jag att min mamma stod och bäddede is sängkammeren, fönstret stod öppet och fäför hordes kyrkklockornas ringanda. Frän den stora Telefunken-radio hördes utsändningen om Tysklands kapitulation. Min mamma sa:
—Nu är det äntligen stut.'

Inga Davidson-Friberg, 'Krigsminnen', in ArkivCentrum Örebro län (ed.), *Örebro 1945* (Örebro, 2007), p. 189.

'cancerous tumor in our nation': Prime Minister's radio address, dated 27 June 1945, in *Keesings Historisch* Archief, vol. 1945, 6345–9. Quoted in Peter Romijn, '"Restoration of Confidence": The Purge of Local Government in the Netherlands as a Problem of Postwar

Reconstruction', in István Deák, Jan T. Gross, and Tony Judt (eds), *The Politics of Retribution in Europe: World War II and Its Aftermath* (Princeton, 2000), p. 186.

'any transfers that take place should be effected in an orderly and humane manner': Potsdam Agreement. Protocol of the Proceedings at Potsdam, 1 August 1945, XII. Orderly Transfer of German Populations.

'how demoralized these people are': StAPM [Siftung Archiv der Parteien und Massenorganisationen der DDR im Bundesarchiv], NL 182/852, fo. 203: 'Bericht', gez. Marg. Schulchen, 15 October 1945.

'And this time, so it appears, ...': quoted in Manfred Overesch, *Das besetzte Deutschland 1945-1947: Eine Tageschronik der Politik, Wirtschaft, Kultur* (Augsburg, 1992), p. 121.

Chapter 3: Life after death: societies of survivors

'Lutz Niethammer...':has observed Lutz Niethammer, 'Erfahrungen und Strukturen: Prolegomena zu einer Geschichte der Gesellschaft der DDR', in Hartmut Kaelble, Jürgen Kocka, and Hartmut Zwahr (eds), *Sozialgeschichte der DDR* (Stuttgart, 1994), p. 100.

'a grand and tragic agent in forming the single-parent family': Irena Krzywicka, 'Kryzys malieiistwa? Ale jakiego?', *Nowa Kultura*, 1956, p. 2. Quoted in Malgorzata Fidelis, 'Equality through Protection: The Politics of Women's Employment in Postwar Poland, 1945-1956', *Slavic Review*, vol. 63, no. 2 (2004), p. 309.

'in the twenty years that have passed...': Jan Szczepański, *Polish Society* (New York, 1970). Quoted in Clive Emsley (ed.), *Conflict and Stability in Europe* (London, 1979), p. 356.

'The young grew up in Kaliningrad...': Ruth Kibelka, *Ostpreußens Schicksalsjahre 1944-1948* (Berlin, 2000), p. 283.

Chapter 4: New politics—east and west

'whoever occupies a territory...': Milovan Djilas, *Conversations with Stalin* (New York, 1962), p. 114.

'Trotskyist, Titoist, Zionist, bourgeois-nationalist traitors': 'Record of the Court in the penal proceeding concerning the leaders of the anti-state conspiracy, heard before the Senate of the State Court in

Prague, November 20th to the 27th, 1952', in Josefa Slánská, *Report on My Husband* (London, 1969), p. 35.

'no separation between political and police work': Bundesarchiv Berlin Lichterfelde, DO-I-7, No. 101, fos 1–51 (here fo. 4): Hauptabteilung PK—Redaktion—to the Leiter der Haupt-Abt. K, Berlin, 26 September 1949.

'the "happiest barrack" of the socialist camp': Heino Nyyssönen, 'Salami Reconstructed: "Goulash Communism" and Political Culture in Hungary', *Cahiers du monde russe*, vol. 47, nos 1–2 (2006), p. 154.

'so far as is practicable, there shall be uniformity of treatment of the German population throughout Germany': Potsdam Agreement. Protocol of the Proceedings, 1 August 1945.

'the period of dour Christian Democrat rule between 1946 and 1957': Paul Preston, *The Politics of Revenge: Fascism and the Military in Twentieth-Century Spain* (London, 1995), pp. 112–13.

'the rise of the postwar consensus': Dan Stone, *Goodbye to All That? The Story of Europe since 1945* (Oxford, 2014), pp. 15–77.

Chapter 5: Building new societies

'scarcely better than Rome burned down by Nero': Wiesław Sauter, 'Sorgen und Nöte eines Schulmanns', in Beata Halicka (ed.), *'Mein Haus an der Oder': Erinnerungen polnischer Neusielder in Westpolen nach 1945* (Paderborn, 2014), p. 309.

'before the war a thorough renewal of the city seemed a hopeless wish of the city planner': Hans Berlage, 'Grundgedanken der Stadt- und Landesplanung Hamburg', quoted in Jeffry M. Diefendorf, 'Konstanty Gutschow and the Reconstruction of Hamburg', *Central European History*, vol. 18, no. 2 (1985), p. 167.

'The Jerries cleaned out the core of the city, a chaotic mess, and now we can start anew': quoted in Mark Clapson, 'The Global Phoenix: From Destruction to Reconstruction, 1945–60', in *The Blitz Companion: Aerial Warfare, Civilians and the City since 1911* (London, 2019), p. 127.

'a fundamental reorganization': Alfons Leitl, 'Erwägungen und Tatsachen zum deutschen Städte-Anbau', *Frankfurter Hefte*, no. 4 (1946), p. 64. Quoted in Hermann Glaser, *1945—Beginn einer Zukunft: Bericht und Dokumentation* (Frankfurt am Main, 1945), p. 143.

Constitution of the French Fourth Republic: 'The Constitution of 27 October 1946'.

'we have the means to be generous toward those who aren't successful in our complicated society': quoted in M. Donald Hancock, 'The Swedish Welfare State: Prospects and Contradictions', *The Wilson Quarterly*, vol. 1, no. 5 (1977), p. 114.

'the happy conjuncture ... of high economic growth and responsiveness to social and economic needs': Eric Willenz, 'Why Europe Needs the Welfare State', *Foreign Policy*, No. 63 (Summer 1986), p. 90.

Proportion of GDP devoted to social expenditure, 1960–75: László Szamuely, 'The Expansion of the Welfare State: An International Comparison', *Acta Oeconomica*, vol. 42, nos 3/4 (1990), p. 194.

'Once upon a time—not that long ago—there was consensus ...': Walter Korpi, 'Welfare-State Regress in Western Europe: Politics, Institutions, Globalization, and Europeanization', *Annual Review of Sociology*, vol. 29 (2003), p. 589.

'une nouvelle organisation de l'espace': Bernard Marchand, *Paris, histoire d'une ville (XIX - XX siècle)* (Paris, 1993), p. 308.

'for the first time in modern British history ...': Mark Abrams, 'The Home-centred Society', *The Listener*, 26 November 1959, pp. 914–15. Quoted in Claire Langhamer, 'The Meanings of Home in Postwar Britain', *Journal of Contemporary History*, vol. 40, no. 2 (2005), p. 341.

'that one had a toilet and a stove of one's own, that I could cook when I wanted': quoted in Moritz Föllmer, 'Cities of Choice: Elective Affinities and the Transformation of Western European Urbanity from the Mid-1950s to the Early 1980s', *Contemporary European History*, vol. 24, no. 4 (2015), Special Issue: Urban Societies in Europe (November 2015), p. 581.

Chapter 6: From scarcity to plenty

'*les trente glorieuses*': Jean Fourestié, *Les Trente Glorieuses, ou la révolution invisible de 1946 à 1975* (Paris, 1979).

'it was simply fantastic': Michael Wildt, *Vom kleinen Wohlstand: Eine Konsumgeschichte der fünfziger Jahre* (Frankfurt am Main, 1996), p. 121.

'stagflation': the term was coined by the Conservative spokesman on economic issues Iain Macleod, speaking in a House of Commons debate on 17 November 1965. *Hansard*, 17 November 1965, p. 1165. Quoted in Edward Nelson and Kalin Nikolov, 'Monetary Policy and Stagflation in the UK' (Bank of England Working Paper, 2002), p. 9.

'the current employment and growth crisis': Dr Otto Graf Lambsdoff, 'Konzept für eine Politik zur Überwindung der Wachstumsschwäche und zur Bekämpfung der Arbeitslosigkeit', 9 September 1982, *Neue Bonner Depesche* 9/82 (Beilage 'Dokumentation'), pp. 1–11.

'the best society that has ever existed in the world': Harry Schein, a Vienna-born Jew who found refuge in Sweden and who in 1963 founded the Swedish Film Institute, quoted in Gordon F. Sander and Paul Britten Austin, 'Sweden after the Fall', *The Wilson Quarterly*, vol. 20, no. 2 (1996), p. 60.

'the growing material and cultural needs of working people': thus Erich Honecker upon succeeding Walter Ulbricht in 1971, in Jonathan R. Zatlin, *The Currency of Socialism: Money and Political Culture in East Germany* (New York, 2007), p. 67.

Chapter 7: The Cold War, nationalism, and the transformation of European politics

'straitjacket of the Cold War': Martin Conway, 'The Rise and Fall of Western Europe's Democratic Age, 1945–1973', *Contemporary European History*, vol. 13, no. 1 (2004), p. 68.

'pave the way for a European federation': quoted in Ian Kershaw, *Roller-Coaster, Europe 1950–2017* (London, 2019), p. 8.

'stopgap operation to bring confidence and security to our friends overseas': quoted in Tony Judt, *Postwar: A History of Europe since 1945* (London, 2005), p. 249.

'Poland needs friendship with the Soviet Union . . .': Jerrold L. Schecter and Vyacheslav V. Luchkov (eds), *Khrushchev Remembers: The Glasnost Tapes* (Boston, 1990), p. 115.

'Germany will never recognize that Oder–Neisse-Line . . .': quoted in Theo Pirker, *Die Geschichte der Sozialdemokratischen Partei Deutschlands 1945–1964* (Berlin, 1977), p. 43.

'the worldwide wave of protests, rallies, marches, sit-ins, and battles with the police . . .': 1968 preface to Jacek Kuroń and Karol Modzelewski's 1964 'Open Letter to the Party', from George Lavan Weissman (ed.), *Revolutionary Marxist Students in Poland Speak Out (1964–1968)* (New York, 1968), p. 2. Quoted in Philipp Gassert and Martin Klimke, 'Introduction: 1968 from Revolt to Research', in Philipp Grassert and Martin Klimke (eds), *1968: Memories and Legacies of a Global Revolt, Bulletin of the German Historical Institute*, Supplement 6 (2009) (Washington, 2009), p. 5.

Chapter 8: The end of empire and its consequences

'a fundamental step in the creation of an Algerian nation': Jean-Pierre Peyroulou, 'Le Cas de Sétif-Kherrata-Guelma (Mai 1945)' (SciencesPo, Paris, 2008).

'without the Empire, France would be merely a liberated country...': quoted in Elizabeth Buettner, *Europe after Empire: Decolonization, Society, and Culture* (Cambridge, 2016), pp. 123–4.

'the full colonial treatment': Frederick Cooper, 'Reconstructing Empire in British and French Africa', *Past & Present*, 210, Supplement 6 (2011), p. 201.

'allowed the army to be stabbed in the back': quoted in Elizabeth Buettner, *Europe after Empire: Decolonization, Society, and Culture* (Cambridge, 2016), p. 135.

'Algeria is France. And who amongst you, Mesdames and messieurs, would hesitate to employ all methods to preserve France?': quoted in Martin Evans, *Algeria: France's Undeclared War* (Oxford, 2012), p. 124.

'One does not compromise...': quoted in Christopher Paul, Colin P. Clarke, Beth Grill, and Molly Dunigan, *Paths to Victory: Detailed Insurgency Case Studies* (chapter on 'Algerian Independence, 1954–1962') (Santa Monica, Calif., 2013), p. 80.

'would be to protect these French *départements* from Indochina's fate and maintain the integrity of national territory': quoted in Elizabeth Buettner, *Europe after Empire: Decolonization, Society, and Culture* (Cambridge, 2016), pp. 144–5.

'the Indian problem would have to be faced': C. R. Attlee, *As It Happened* (New York, 1954), p. 254.

'Walking along the Boulevard de Belleville...': Brian Fitzpatrick, 'Immigrants', in J. E. Flower (ed.), *France Today: Introductory Studies* (London and New York, 4th edn, 1980), pp. 96–7.

'Commonwealth migration, as a permanent legacy of empire, had created a multiracial Britain and religious pluralism': Stuart Hall, 'The Local and the Global: Globalization and Ethnicity', in A. McClintock, A. Mufti, and E. Shohat (eds), *Dangerous Liaisons: Gender, Nation, and Postcolonial Perspectives* (Minneapolis, 1997), p. 176. Quoted in Wendy Webster, 'The Empire Comes Home: Commonwealth Migration to Britain', in Andrew Thompson (ed.), *Britain's Experience of Empire in the Twentieth Century* (Oxford, 2012), pp. 128, 159.

'Chicken Tikka Masala is now the true British national dish...': 'Robin Cook's chicken tikka masala speech', *The Guardian*, 19 April 2001.

'might be rather swamped by people with a different culture': quoted in Paul Kelso, 'Floods, Inundation, and Other Unspeakable Words', *The Guardian*, 25 April 2002.

'She killed the National Front that night...': Fraser Nelson, 'How Maggie's "swamped" Comment Crushed the National Front', *The Spectator*, 29 October 2014.

Chapter 9: Postwar cultures

'a landmark of the integration of urban planning traditions...': UNESCO, World Heritage Convention, 'Le Havre, the City Rebuilt by Auguste Perret', <https://whc.unesco.org/en/list/1181>.

'city of twentieth-century people': Rein Blijstra, in *Het Vrije Volk* 13 November 1952. Quoted in 'Post-War Reconstruction Community Rotterdam', <https://wederopbouwrotterdam.nl/en/articles/post-war-reconstruction>. Blijstra (1901–75) was a journalist and culture editor of *Het Vrije Volk* from 1945 until 1966; from 1951 to 1959 he was also the editor of *Forum: Maandblad voor architectuur en gebonden kunsten.*

'an essential element of the socialist cultural revolution': Walther Ulbricht, quoted in Paul Betts, 'The Twilight of the Idols', *The Journal of Modern History*, vol. 72, no. 3 (2000), p. 756.

'THE superstar in the Fifties and Sixties': Promipool, 'Schlagerstar Freddy Quinn–So geht es ihm heute', <https://www.promipool.de/stars/schlagerstar-freddy-quinn-so-geht-ihm-heute> (accessed 3 June 2022).

'they *looked* different': Tony Judt, *Postwar: A History of Europe since 1945* (London, 2005), p. 348.

'melancholy tangos and vulgar foxtrots': *Komsomol'skaia Pravda*, 8 December 1951.

'jazz-style dance music': Gleb Tsipursky, 'Jazz, Power, and Soviet Youth in the Early Cold War, 1948–1953', *The Journal of Musicology*, vol. 33, no. 3 (2016), pp. 339–40.

'nonculture': 'Appell an den Urmenschen', *Berliner Zeitung*, 13 December 1956. Cited in Uta G. Poiger, 'Rock n' Roll, Female Sexuality and the Cold War Battle over German Identities', *Journal of Modern History*, vol. 68, no. 3 (1996), p. 577.

'the most successful rock band in Hungarian history': see <https://www.allmusic.com/artist/omega-mn0001073347/biography> (accessed 6 June 2022). Generally, see Timothy Ryback, *Rock around the Bloc: A History of Rock Music in Eastern Europe and the Soviet Union* (New York, 1990).

Chapter 10: When did the postwar era end?

'As events of the Second World War recede...': Sarah Farmer, *Martyred Village: Commemorating the 1944 Massacre at Oradour-sur-Glane* (Berkeley, Los Angeles, and London, 1999), pp. 212–13.

'The war is too far from me. Me and nobody in my family has experienced something during that time': quoted in Huibertha B. Mitima-Verloop, Paul A. Boelen, and Trudy T. M. Mooren, 'The Post-War Generation Remembers: A Mixed-Method Study Exploring Children's Attitudes towards World War II Commemoration', *Children & Society: The International Journal of Childhood and Children's Services*, vol. 36, no. 5 (2022), p. 754.

'When one examines the "return of memories"...': Dan Stone, 'Editor's Introduction: Postwar Europe as History', in Dan Stone (ed.), *The Oxford Handbook of Postwar European History* (Oxford, 2012), p. 33.

Further reading

General

The literature about postwar Europe is vast, and reflects how perspectives on the subject have changed over the past decades. In recent years a number of excellent texts have been published that offer revealing and insightful understandings of the history of Europe as a whole since 1945. Most impressive—and the place that reading about postwar Europe must start—is Tony Judt's magisterial *Postwar: A History of Europe since 1945* (London: William Heinemann, 2005), which reflected the cautious optimism of the time when it was written, some two decades ago. Also indispensable is the excellent collection edited by Dan Stone, *The Oxford Handbook of Postwar European History* (Oxford: Oxford University Press, 2012; paperback, Oxford, 2014). Dan Stone has also authored a fine if less optimistic general history of postwar Europe, structured around what he saw as the rise and fall of the 'postwar consensus', *Goodbye to All That? The Story of Europe since 1945* (Oxford: Oxford University Press, 2014). Ian Kershaw's more recent, sober, and thoroughly reliable text, *Roller-Coaster: Europe 1950–2017* (London: Allen Lane, 2018), also takes a somewhat less optimistic view, ending with a chapter on 'Crisis Years' and an afterword entitled 'A New Era of Insecurity'. (Kershaw examined the Europe of the late 1940s in his earlier volume, *To Hell and Back: Europe 1914–1949* (London: Allen

Lane, 2015)). A further solid, detailed survey of postwar Europe is that by Tom Buchanan, *Europe's Troubled Peace: 1945 to the Present* (2nd edn, Oxford: John Wiley & Sons, 2012). Also useful, if representative of a more optimistic time, is the collection edited by Mary Fulbrook, *Europe since 1945 (Short Oxford History of Europe)* (Oxford: Oxford University Press, 2001). Reference also should be made to the very good collection edited by Klaus Larres, *A Companion to Europe since 1945* (Chichester: Wiley-Blackwell, 2009).

There also are important volumes that address the history of Europe's 20th century as a whole and, accordingly, examine the second half of the period. Among the most notable of these is Mark Mazower's widely praised *Dark Continent: Europe's Twentieth Century* (London: Allen Lane, 1998). A particularly stimulating, if somewhat idiosyncratic, approach is that of Richard Vinen, *A History in Fragments: Europe in the Twentieth Century* (London: Little, Brown and Company, 2000). Also see the exhaustive text by Bernard Wasserstein, *Barbarism and Civilization: A History of Europe in Our Time* (Oxford: Oxford University Press, 2007). An innovative approach is that taken by Dan Diner in *Cataclysms: A History of the Twentieth Century from Europe's Edge* (Madison, Wis.: University of Wisconsin Press, 2008). An insightful discussion of the role of the military in 20th-century European society may be found in James J. Sheehan, *Where Have All the Soldiers Gone? The Transformation of Modern Europe* (Boston and New York: Houghton Mifflin Harcourt, 2009). Very useful is T. C. W. Blanning (ed.), *The Oxford Illustrated History of Modern Europe* (Oxford and New York: Oxford University Press, 1996). Finally, while it was written over three decades ago and its scope spans not just Europe but the globe, Eric Hobsbawm's *Age of Extremes: The Short Twentieth Century 1914–1991* (London: Michael Joseph, 1994) remains an impressive source of insights into the history of postwar Europe.

The end of the Second World War

Richard Bessel, *Germany 1945: From War to Peace* (London: HarperCollins, 2009).

István Deák, Jan T. Gross, and Tony Judt (eds), *The Politics of Retribution in Europe: World War II and Its Aftermath* (Princeton: Princeton University Press, 2000).

Jon Elster (ed.), *Retribution and Reparation in the Transition to Democracy* (Cambridge: Cambridge University Press, 2006).

Keith Lowe, *Savage Continent: Europe in the Aftermath of World War II* (London: Penguin, 2013).

Norman M. Naimark, *The Russians in Germany: A History of the Soviet Zone of Occupation* (Cambridge, Mass.: Harvard University Press, 1995).

Societies of refugees and survivors

Richard Bessel, *Germany 1945: From War to Peace* (London: HarperCollins, 2009).

Richard Bessel and Dirk Schumann (eds), *Life after Death: Approaches to a Cultural and Social History of Europe During the 1940s and 1950s* (Cambridge: Cambridge University Press, 2003).

Frank Biess and Robert G. Moeller (eds), *Histories of the Aftermath: The Legacies of the Second World War in Europe* (New York and Oxford: Berghahn, 2010).

Robert Dale, *Demobilised Veterans in Late Stalinist Leningrad: Soldiers to Civilians* (London: Bloomsbury Academic, 2015).

Peter Gatrell, *The Unsettling of Europe: The Great Migration, 1945 to the Present* (London: Allen Lane, 2019).

Robert G. Moeller, *War Stories: The Search for a Usable Past in the Federal Republic of Germany* (Berkeley, Los Angeles, and London: University of California Press, 2001).

Norman M. Naimark, *The Russians in Germany: A History of the Soviet Zone of Occupation* (Cambridge, Mass.: Harvard University Press, 1995).

Norman M. Naimark, *Fires of Hatred: Ethnic Cleansing in Twentieth Century Europe* (Cambridge, Mass., and London: Harvard University Press, 2002).

Jessica Reinisch and Elizabeth White (eds), *The Disentanglement of Populations: Migration, Expulsion and Displacement in Postwar Europe, 1944–49* (Basingstoke: Palgrave Macmillan, 2011).

New politics—east and west

Anne Applebaum, *Iron Curtain: The Crushing of Eastern Europe 1944–56* (London: Penguin Books, 2013).

François Fejtö, *A History of the People's Democracies: Eastern Europe since Stalin* (Harmondsworth: Penguin Books, 1974).

Melvyn P. Leffler and Odd Arne Westad (eds), *The Cambridge History of the Cold War. Volume 1: Origins* (Cambridge: Cambridge University Press, 2010).

Martin McCauley (ed.), *Communist Power in Europe 1944–1949* (London: Macmillan, 1977).

Norman M. Naimark, *Stalin and the Fate of Europe: The Postwar Struggle for Sovereignty* (Cambridge, Mass., and London: Harvard University Press, 2019).

John W. Young, *Cold War Europe 1945–1991* (2nd edn, London: Hodder, 1996).

Building new societies

Gerold Ambrosius and William H. Hubbard, *A Social and Economic History of Twentieth-Century Europe* (Cambridge, Mass., and London: Harvard University Press, 1989).

Mark Clapson, 'The Global Phoenix: From Destruction to Reconstruction, 1945–60', in Mark Clapson, *The Blitz Companion: Aerial Warfare, Civilians and the City since 1911* (London: University of Westminster Press, 2019).

Jeffry M. Diefendorf, 'Urban Reconstruction in Europe after World War II', *Urban Studies*, vol. 26, no. 1 (1989), pp. 128–43.

Claire Duchen and Irene-Bandhauer-Schöffmann (eds), *When the War Was Over: Women, War and Peace in Europe, 1940–1956* (London and New York: Leicester University Press, 2000).

Peter Hennessy, *Never Again: Britain 1945–51* (London: Jonathan Cape, 1992).

Mark Mazower, Jessica Reinisch, and David Feldman (eds), *Post-War Reconstruction in Europe: International Perspectives, 1945–1949* (Oxford: Oxford University Press, 2011).

Alfred C. Mierzejewski, *The Party's Over: The End of the Welfare State Boom in Western Europe* (Lanham, Md., and London: Lexington Books, 2021).

Nationalism, democracy, and postwar politics

Frank Biess, *German Angst: Fear and Democracy in the Federal Republic of Germany* (Oxford: Oxford University Press, 2020).

Martin Conway, 'The Rise and Fall of Western Europe's Democratic Age, 1945–1973', *Contemporary European History*, vol. 13, no. 1 (2004), pp. 67–88.

Martin Conway, *Western Europe's Democratic Age: 1945–1968* (Princeton: Princeton University Press, 2020).

André Gerrits, *Nationalism in Europe since 1945* (London: Bloomsbury Academic, 2016).

From scarcity to plenty

Andrea Boltho (ed.), *The European Economy: Growth and Crisis* (Oxford: Oxford University Press, 1982).

Alec Cairncross, *Years of Recovery: British Economic Policy 1945–51* (London: Methuen, 1985).

Victoria de Grazia, *Irresistible Empire: America's Advance through Twentieth-Century Europe* (Cambridge, Mass., and London: Harvard University Press, 2005).

Barry Eichengreen, *The European Economy since 1945: Coordinated Capitalism and Beyond* (Princeton: Princeton University Press, 2007).

Sandra Halperin, *War and Social Change in Modern Europe: The Great Transformation Revisited* (Cambridge: Cambridge University Press, 2004).

Alan S. Milward, *The Reconstruction of Western Europe 1945–51* (Berkeley and Los Angeles: University of California Press, 1984).

W. Rand Smith, *The Left's Dirty Job: The Politics of Industrial Restructuring in France and Spain* (Pittsburgh: University of Pittsburgh Press, 1998).

Simon Usherwood and John Pinder, *The European Union: A Very Short Introduction* (4th edn, Oxford: Oxford University Press, 2018).

The end of empire and its consequences

Christopher Bayly and Tim Harper, *Forgotten Wars: The End of Britain's Asian Empire* (London: Allen Lane, 2007).

Elizabeth Buettner, *Europe after Empire: Decolonization, Society, and Culture* (Cambridge: Cambridge University Press, 2016).

Robert Gildea, *Empires of the Mind: The Colonial Past and the Politics of the Present* (Cambridge: Cambridge University Press, 2019).

Dane Kennedy, *Decolonization: A Very Short Introduction* (Oxford: Oxford University Press, 2016).

Martin Thomas and Andrew S. Thompson (eds), *The Oxford Handbook of the Ends of Empire* (Oxford: Oxford University Press, 2018).

Postwar cultures

Paul Betts, *Ruin and Renewal: Civilising Europe after the Second World War* (London: Profile Books, 2020).

Victoria de Grazia, *Irresistible Empire: America's Advance through Twentieth-Century Europe* (Cambridge, Mass., and London: Harvard University Press, 2005).

Axel Schildt and Detlef Siegfried (eds), *Between Marx and Coca-Cola: Youth Cultures and Changing European Society, 1960–1980* (New York and Oxford: Berghahn Books, 1999).

Hanna Schissler (ed.), *The Miracle Years: A Cultural History of Western Germany, 1949–1968* (Princeton: Princeton University Press, 2001).

Bernard Wasserstein, *Vanishing Diaspora: The Jews in Europe since 1945* (London: Penguin Books, 1997).

Paul Wood, Francis Frascina, Jonahan Harris, and Charles Harrison, *Modernism in Dispute: Art since the Forties* (New Haven and London: Yale University Press, 1993).

Some single-country accounts

Norman Davies, *God's Playground: A History of Poland. Volume II: 1795 to the Present* (Oxford: Oxford University Press, 1981).

Robert Gildea, *France since 1945* (Oxford: Oxford University Press, 2002).

Paul Ginsborg, *A History of Contemporary Italy, 1943–1980* (London: Penguin Books, 2003).

Paul Ginsborg, *Italy and Its Discontents: Family, Civil Society, State, 1980–2001* (London: Penguin Books, 2003).

Ulrich Herbert, *A History of Twentieth-Century Germany* (Oxford: Oxford University Press, 2019).

Arthur Marwick, *British Society since 1945* (London: Penguin, 1990).

Robert G. Moeller (ed.), *West Germany under Construction: Politics, Society and Culture in the Adenauer Era* (Ann Arbor: University of Michigan Press, 1997).

Pól O'Dochartaigh, *Germany since 1945* (Basingstoke: Palgrave Macmillan, 2004).

Paul Preston, *The Triumph of Democracy in Spain* (London: Methuen, 1986).

Paul Preston, *The Politics of Revenge: Fascism and the Military in Twentieth-Century Spain* (London: Routledge, 1995).

Karl Schlögel, *Ukraine: A Nation on the Borderland* (London: Reaktion Books: 2018).

Frank Trentmann, *Out of the Darkness: The Germans, 1942–2022* (London: Allen Lane, 2023).

Richard Vinen, *France, 1934–1970* (Basingstoke and London: Macmillan, 1996).

Steven F. White, *Modern Italy's Founding Fathers: The Making of a Postwar Republic* (London: Bloomsbury Academic, 2020).

Index

Q

R

Index

Index

DIPLOMACY
A Very Short Introduction
Joseph M. Siracusa

Like making war, diplomacy has been around a very long time, at least since the Bronze Age. It was primitive by today's standards, there were few rules, but it was a recognizable form of diplomacy. Since then, diplomacy has evolved greatly, coming to mean different things, to different persons, at different times, ranging from the elegant to the inelegant. Whatever one's definition, few could doubt that the course and consequences of the major events of modern international diplomacy have shaped and changed the global world in which we live. Joseph M. Siracusa introduces the subject of diplomacy from a historical perspective, providing examples from significant historical phases and episodes to illustrate the art of diplomacy in action.

'Professor Siracusa provides a lively introduction to diplomacy through the perspective of history.'
Gerry Woodard, Senior Fellow in Political Science at the University of Melbourne and former Australasian Ambassador in Asia

www.oup.com/vsi

INTERNATIONAL RELATIONS
A Very Short Introduction
Paul Wilkinson

Of undoubtable relevance today, in a post-9-11 world of growing political tension and unease, this *Very Short Introduction* covers the topics essential to an understanding of modern international relations. Paul Wilkinson explains the theories and the practice that underlies the subject, and investigates issues ranging from foreign policy, arms control, and terrorism, to the environment and world poverty. He examines the role of organizations such as the United Nations and the European Union, as well as the influence of ethnic and religious movements and terrorist groups which also play a role in shaping the way states and governments interact. This up-to-date book is required reading for those seeking a new perspective to help untangle and decipher international events.

GEOPOLITICS
A Very Short Introduction
Klaus Dodds

In certain places such as Iraq or Lebanon, moving a few feet either side of a territorial boundary can be a matter of life or death, dramatically highlighting the connections between place and politics. For a country's location and size as well as its sovereignty and resources all affect how the people that live there understand and interact with the wider world. Using wide-ranging examples, from historical maps to James Bond films and the rhetoric of political leaders like Churchill and George W. Bush, this Very Short Introduction shows why, for a full understanding of contemporary global politics, it is not just smart - it is essential - to be geopolitical.

'Engrossing study of a complex topic.'

Mick Herron, Geographical.

GLOBAL ECONOMIC HISTORY

A Very Short Introduction

Robert C. Allen

Why are some countries rich and others poor? In 1500, the income differences were small, but they have grown dramatically since Columbus reached America. Since then, the interplay between geography, globalization, technological change, and economic policy has determined the wealth and poverty of nations. The industrial revolution was Britain's path breaking response to the challenge of globalization. Western Europe and North America joined Britain to form a club of rich nations by pursuing four polices: creating a national market by abolishing internal tariffs and investing in transportation, erecting an external tariff to protect their fledgling industries from British competition, banks to stabilize the currency and mobilize domestic savings for investment, and mass education to prepare people for industrial work.

Together these countries pioneered new technologies that have made them ever richer. Before the Industrial Revolution, most of the world's manufacturing was done in Asia, but industries from Casablanca to Canton were destroyed by western competition in the nineteenth century, and Asia was transformed into 'underdeveloped countries' specializing in agriculture. The spread of economic development has been slow since modern technology was invented to fit the needs of rich countries and is ill adapted to the economic and geographical conditions of poor countries. A few countries—Japan, Soviet Russia, South Korea, Taiwan, and perhaps China—have, nonetheless, caught up with the West through creative responses to the technological challenge and with Big Push industrialization that has achieved rapid growth through investment coordination. Whether other countries can emulate the success of East Asia is a challenge for the future.

www.oup.com/vsi

THE UNITED NATIONS
A Very Short Introduction
Jussi M. Hanhimäki

With this much-needed introduction to the UN, Jussi Hanhimäki engages the current debate over the organization's effectiveness as he provides a clear understanding of how it was originally conceived, how it has come to its present form, and how it must confront new challenges in a rapidly changing world. After a brief history of the United Nations and its predecessor, the League of Nations, the author examines the UN's successes and failures as a guardian of international peace and security, as a promoter of human rights, as a protector of international law, and as an engineer of socio-economic development.

www.oup.com/vsi

LAW
A Very Short Introduction
Raymond Wacks

Law underlies our society - it protects our rights, imposes duties on each of us, and establishes a framework for the conduct of almost every social, political, and economic activity. The punishment of crime, compensation of the injured, and the enforcement of contracts are merely some of the tasks of a modern legal system. It also strives to achieve justice, promote freedom, and protect our security. This *Very Short Introduction* provides a clear, jargon-free account of modern legal systems, explaining how the law works both in the Western tradition and around the world.

www.oup.com/vsi

LEADERSHIP
A Very Short Introduction
Keith Grint

In this *Very Short Introduction* Keith Grint prompts the reader to rethink their understanding of what leadership is. He examines the way leadership has evolved from its earliest manifestations in ancient societies, highlighting the beginnings of leadership writings through Plato, Sun Tzu, Machiavelli and others, to consider the role of the social, economic, and political context undermining particular modes of leadership. Exploring the idea that leaders cannot exist without followers, and recognising that we all have diverse experiences and assumptions of leadership, Grint looks at the practice of management, its history, future, and influence on all aspects of society.

www.oup.com/vsi

Economics
A Very Short Introduction
Partha Dasgupta

Economics has the capacity to offer us deep insights into some of the most formidable problems of life, and offer solutions to them too. Combining a global approach with examples from everyday life, Partha Dasgupta describes the lives of two children who live very different lives in different parts of the world: in the Mid-West USA and in Ethiopia. He compares the obstacles facing them, and the processes that shape their lives, their families, and their futures. He shows how economics uncovers these processes, finds explanations for them, and how it forms policies and solutions.

> 'An excellent introduction . . . presents mathematical and statistical findings in straightforward prose.'
>
> **Financial Times**

MODERNISM
A Very Short Introduction
Christopher Butler

Whether we recognise it or not, virtually every aspect of our
life today has been influenced in part by the aesthetic legacy
of Modernism. In this *Very Short Introduction* Christopher Butler
examines how and why Modernism began, explaining what
it is and showing how it has gradually informed all aspects of
20th and 21st century life. Butler considers several aspects
of modernism including some modernist works; movements
and notions of the avant garde; and the idea of 'progress' in art.
Butler looks at modernist ideas of the self, subjectivity,
irrationalism, people and machines, and political definitions
of modernism as a whole.

www.oup.com/vsi

THE FIRST WORLD WAR
A Very Short Introduction
Michael Howard

By the time the First World War ended in 1918, eight million people had died in what had been perhaps the most apocalyptic episode the world had known. This *Very Short Introduction* provides a concise and insightful history of the 'Great War', focusing on why it happened, how it was fought, and why it had the consequences it did. It examines the state of Europe in 1914 and the outbreak of war; the onset of attrition and crisis; the role of the US; the collapse of Russia; and the weakening and eventual surrender of the Central Powers. Looking at the historical controversies surrounding the causes and conduct of war, Michael Howard also describes how peace was ultimately made, and the potent legacy of resentment left to Germany.

'succinct, comprehensive and beautifully written. Indeed reading it is an experience comparable to scanning the clues of a well-composed crossword puzzle. Every allusion is eventually supplied with an answer, and the finished product defies the puzzler's disbelief that the intricacies can be brought to a convincing conclusion.... Michael Howard is the master of the short book'

TLS

2 04

www.oup.com/vsi